Perennials
for bed and border

STIRLING MACOBOY
Perennials
for bed and border

LANSDOWNE
Sydney Auckland London New York

Published by Lansdowne Press, Sydney
A division of RPLA Pty Limited
176 South Creek Road, Dee Why West, N.S.W.
Australia 2099

First published 1983
Reprinted 1986
© Copyright Stirling Macoboy 1983
Produced in Australia

Typeset in Australia by V.I.P. Typesetters,
397 Riley Street, Surry Hills, N.S.W. 2010
Printed in Hong Kong
by South China Printing Co.
Designed by Jim Paton
Line drawings by Murray Frederick
Edited by Sue Wagner

**National Library of Australia
Cataloguing-in-Publication Data**

Macoboy, Stirling, 1927- ,
Perennials for bed and border,
Includes index.
ISBN 0 7018 1720 8
1. Perennials (Plants). 1. Title.
635.9'32

*For Jack Lee,
who grows them well.*

ACKNOWLEDGMENTS

Not all plants illustrated in this book may be
available in every country in which it is sold.
Some may even be restricted. *Cynara* and
Onopordon for instance are classed as noxious
weeds in Western Australia. The flowers were
photographed in many different gardens in many
different countries.

In the United States
At the Strybing Arboretum, San Francisco;
the U.C.L.A. Botanic Garden, Los Angeles;
the Brooklyn Botanic Garden, New York;
Los Angeles State and County Arboretum,
Arcadia; the Huntington Gardens, San Marino,
Calif.; the Santa Barbara Botanic Garden, Calif.

In France
At the Parc des Floralies, Vincennes; the Jardin
Botanique de Paris.

In Australia
At the National Botanic Garden, Canberra,
A.C.T.; the Brisbane Botanic Garden; the Royal
Botanic Gardens, Sydney; the Waterhouse
Camellia Garden, Yowie Bay, N.S.W.; Milton
Park and Retford Park, Bowral, N.S.W.; Lindfield
Park, Mt Wilson, N.S.W.; St Bernard Hotel,
Mt Tamborine, Qld; Hyde Park, Sydney and
Seppeltsfield, S.A.

In England
At the R.H.S. Garden, Wisley; Spalding, Lincs.;
the Royal Botanic Garden, Kew; the Chelsea
Flower Show; Hidcote, Gloucs.; the Hillier
Arboretum; Syon Park, London; the Oxford
Botanic Garden; the Beth Chatto Garden, Essex.

In Ireland
At the Irish National Botanic Garden, Glasnevin;
St Stephen's Green and Merrion Square, all in
Dublin; Garinish, Inniskillen, Co. Cork.

In Asia
At the Hong Kong Botanic Garden and Tokyo
Botanic Garden.

Many species were photographed in my own
garden and those of friends. My thanks to the
volunteer notetakers and chauffeurs without
whom many of the pictures would have remained
untaken.

PHOTOGRAPHS

Half Title page: Meconopsis grandis,
Blue Tibetan Poppy.
Title page: Massed planting of *Astilbe* X *arendsii,*
Parc des Floralies, Paris.
Opposite Page: The Bog Garden at Wisley features
naturalized plantings of moisture-loving perennials

CONTENTS

Introduction — What is a perennial?

Setting out to divide the world's flora into convenient classifications for the home gardener, some difficulties in definition become apparent.

This is particularly true of the perennials, which form the largest classification of all. The word 'perennial' is simply a form of the Latin *perennis,* meaning something that survives through a number of years. That easily rules out the annual flowers that grow, flower and die in a single season, and the biennials as well. But it still seems to leave all other types of plant in the perennial classification: trees, shrubs, climbers, bulbs, epiphytes, cacti, ferns, conifers, palms, in fact everything in the garden, lovely and otherwise.

But as we are home gardeners and not pedants, we can subtract the trees (including the palms and conifers), the climbers and most of the shrubs as well. Certainly they are *perennial,* but they are also bigger, *woodier* plants than we have in mind in our classification. They are somehow *permanent* in a way that other perennial plants are not. Cacti and ferns are obviously in recognizable classes of

their own; so they can go too, as can the epiphytes and most of the spring bulbs which are with us for such a short time each year that the word 'perennial' doesn't seem to cover them at all.

So what are we left with? Still a very large grouping of plants, mostly without definite woody stems and branches, and mostly dying back either to fleshy roots or to an evergreen crown at the end of their flowering season.

These are the true perennials; the border or accent plants: the mainstay of any garden display, year in and year out. They may vary in height from a few centimetres to as much as 4 metres, and by definition as perennial, the majority of them will flower and spread for as long as the gardener takes an interest in them and gives them the care they need — which is certainly less time-consuming than the care of annuals and biennials.

For convenience only, garden perennials are often divided into three types:

1. *The Shrubby Perennials* or sub-shrubs such as *Helianthemum, Calceolaria, Aurinia,* Heliotrope, Marguerite daisies,

Midsummer bloom in the perennial borders at Garinish, County Cork, makes a rainbow of colour

A border of red and purple flowering perennials at famous Hidcote, Gloucestershire

Osteospermum and *Pelargoniums*. These have persistent branches of a less woody type than true shrubs, and are normally trimmed back at the end of the flowering season. Many gardeners prefer to start them afresh from cuttings every year or two.

2. The *Hardy Herbaceous Perennials*. These include most of the familiar border plants such as *Acanthus, Ajuga, Campanula,* Hellebores, Peonies, perennial phlox and both the Michaelmas and Shasta daisies. All of them are native to cold climates and while their rootstock lives on from year to year, the leafy or herbaceous top growth usually dies down in autumn. Most of these plants spread by means of underground suckers which develop after flowering. Herbaceous perennials are not so long-lived in warmer climates, where continuous growth, brought on by the lack of a real winter resting season, seems to exhaust their vitality.

3. *Perennials with rhizomes or tubers.* These are the subject of a separate book in this series, for they are mostly native to warmer climates than the herbaceous perennials and are used as an alternative to them in sub-tropical areas. They include *Agapanthus, Begonias, Cannas, Dietes,* most of the *Gesneriads,* Gingers, Kangaroo Paws, *Spathiphyllums* and many other Aroids. In temperate areas these are useful in a mixed border to help avoid a bare effect in winter. Some may be grown in cold areas, but they develop an herbaceous habit as their tops are cut down by frost.

Larger herbaceous perennials are often planted among shrubs or used as feature plants to break the monotonous lines of annual beds.

Smaller perennials may be used to soften the hard lines between paths and lawns: as marginal plants around ponds and streams and to disguise or emphasize changes of level in many garden layouts.

On following pages we show you many ways to use all of these exciting and spectacular plants.

Stirling Macoboy
Neutral Bay, N.S.W.

7

Perennials — Ways to use them

1. *Light up a corner of your terrace with tubs full of showy Marguerite daisies. Pinch out growth to stimulate branching and feed well when flower buds form. With regular dead-heading, the display will continue for months.*

2. *Common zonal geraniums make a grand display when planted in half-barrels along a driveway or against a blank wall. They'll need plenty of sun, a well-drained soil mix and regular spraying against caterpillars. Watch for rust and don't over-water.*

1

2

4

5

3. Soften the hard edges of a flight of steps with trailing perennials such as Aurinia, Corydalis *(illustrated)*, Helianthemum or violets. Snip back hard when flowering's over to avoid legginess.

4. On a semi-shaded bank with cool, moist soil, you can extend the colour display of Azaleas for months with showy Astilbe and Primula species. Add foliage interest with variegated Hostas, but be sure to lay plenty of snail bait.

5. Along a sun-drenched pathway in gravelly well-drained soil, you can plant a dazzling border of miniature alpine perennials such as white Arabis, golden Aurinia and multi-coloured alpine phlox. Underplant with dwarf spring bulbs such as Hoop Petticoats, Crocus species, Grape Hyacinths and Lachenalias.

6. Site spectacular water-loving perennials around the margin of a garden pool. Here are Iris, Astilbe, Primula and Arum lilies. Other possibilities are Alchemilla and Ligularia.

3

6

Perennials — How to plant and grow them

Perennials, as observed earlier, may be used as feature plants, among shrubs, as edgings for paths and pools — in fact anywhere you like.

Their traditional landscaping use, however, is in the creation of perennial borders, an eye-catching system for plant display developed in the late 19th century.

Perennial or herbaceous borders are long beds of flowering plants planned in such a way that the soil is never completely bare. The plants are chosen both for the colour of their flowers and for the decorative value of their foliage, and arranged so that there is always a variety of flower colour in every part of the growing season.

The most popular plants used for this work bloom regularly for several months of every year, and need replanting or dividing only at four or five year intervals. Their range of form and colour is almost endless, as this book sets out to show.

Planning and planting so the cycle of growth and bloom takes place continuously is one of the more challenging aspects of making a border. Long or short, wide or narrow, in sun or in shade, the border of mixed perennial plants can reflect the likes and dislikes of its creator as no other form of garden can. Those with a liking for vivid colour can have a living rainbow for months on end. Those with less flamboyant tastes may prefer to make a border that blooms all in a single colour — all pink, or all blue or all yellow. Even one in which all the plants have grey or silver leaves.

Many perennials have interesting leaf-forms too, and careful planning by leaf texture and colour can give a delightful result.

The perennial border is a style of gardening very popular in Europe, but rarely seen in the southern hemisphere, where many of the traditional plants used north of the equator are not seen at their best. This lack of enthusiasm is hard to understand. Precisely because of their milder climate, southern hemisphere gardeners have a decided advantage in the wealth of plant material they can choose from, and a much longer period for peak display.

Perennial borders are quite easy to maintain. Once the soil is properly prepared and the planting carried out according to plan, they look after themselves for years on end. Dead-heading to promote bloom, cutting back after the flowers have died away and providing a generous dose of fertilizer in late winter are the only regular chores until the plants have spread so thickly that they must be divided and replanted. But this will be only every four years at the most.

SELECTING A SITE

The first move in planning a perennial border is to select the most suitable site and surroundings. Aspect is relatively unimportant, though a border running from north to south ensures even exposure to sunlight for all the plants. The site should be flat, sheltered and preferably in a sunny position on well-drained soil, away from tree roots.

a: *New perennial growth can be supported with branched twigs.*

b: *'Deadhead' perennials by regularly cutting faded flowers.*

c: *In autumn, perennials are cut back almost to ground level.*

The length of a perennial border will be determined by the size of your garden, but at least 10m (30ft) is desirable. The minimum width is about 1.5m (4½ft), and the ideal two or three times as wide as this, with a working path either at the back or in the centre if the border is to be double-sided. The border can be rectangular and straight, single or double, in a long, sweeping curve, or planned with scalloped edges.

If it is absolutely necessary that the border be in the open without a wall or shrub background, it should be planned so that the taller plants are in the centre of the bed, with others graduated down from them on either side. Normally, of course, the taller plants are placed at the back.

PREPARING THE BED

As your perennial bed or border will be densely planted, and most of the plants won't be disturbed for years, it is important to prepare the soil correctly. It won't be possible to make changes later without disturbing the entire display.

First, dig over the border site from end to end at least spade deep, thoroughly break up the soil and remove all roots of trees and perennial weeds. Dig in plenty of farmyard manure, compost, blood and bone and chemical fertilizer and turn over again.

If the site is inclined to be damp and soggy, a layer of coke and coarse sand can be dug in deep down as the bed is trenched. If the soil is too light, vegetable compost is the best addition. Spent mushroom compost is quite cheap, and peatmoss is economical bought in 50kg (1cwt) amounts from your local nursery. At least 10cm (4in) of it worked into the entire bed makes a rich, moisture-retaining

A perennial border at Milton Park, Bowral, N.S.W., is planted in a rainbow of colour

supplement to the soil which will benefit your perennial plants for years on end.

Lime, preferably in the form of dolomite, may be dug in at the same time, but not too much of it. Many perennials are acid-loving. Better to add the lime as individual clumps go in. You'll find which species need it in individual book entries.

After planting, bone meal is the best

d: *An entire perennial clump can be lifted with a garden fork.*

e: *Smaller clumps can be divided by levering apart with two forks.*

f: *Perennials should be planted in clumps, rather than singly.*

BACK

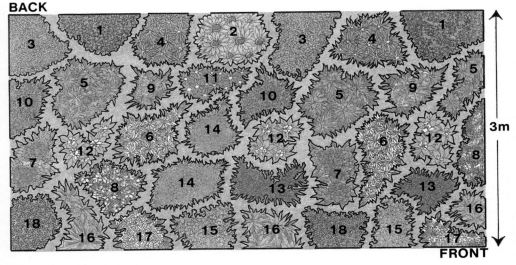

3m

FRONT

Section of 3m deep perennial border

1. **Macleaya,** reddish, summer
2. **Helianthus,** yellow, summer
3. **Solidago,** yellow, autumn
4. **Aster,** mauve, autumn
5. **Delphinium,** blue, summer
6. **Shasta Daisy,** white, summer
7. **Peony,** red, spring
8. **Gypsophila,** white, spring
9. **Iris,** blue, spring
10. **Rudbeckia,** orange, summer
11. **Rudbeckia,** orange, summer
12. **Euphorbia,** lime green, summer
13. **Penstemon,** red, autumn
14. **Astilbe,** pink, summer
15. **Pinks,** pink, spring
16. **Aurinia,** yellow, spring
17. **Arabis,** white, spring
18. **Phlox,** mauve, spring

---

fertilizer; it can be applied at any time to individual plant groups.

It is a great advantage if the entire bed can be raised 8cm (3in) or more above the surrounding garden. This will ensure good drainage, which is a must for most perennials.

PLANNING THE DISPLAY

Planning the layout of your perennial border is best done on paper, as shown in the chart overleaf. Using such a chart in conjunction with individual book entries will help you make sure that the tallest plants are at the back of the border and the lowest in the front. There are exceptions to this, of course. Some larger plants with particularly interesting foliage or flowers, such as Paeonies, could well be positioned near the front of the border, where their exquisite colours and perfumes can better be appreciated.

On your own paper plan, work out your colour harmonies with crayons, so all flowers of a certain colour are distributed throughout the border and not in one great clump. Give some thought to a succession of bloom, so that an early-flowering plant is surrounded by others which come out a little later and will fill in the spaces after the early bloomer has been cut back.

The ideal to aim for is that there will be some clumps of plants in bloom all year, and in a variety of colours.

Most favourite perennial plants are summer and autumn bloomers, so this succession of bloom will often be achieved with the addition of large clumps of spring and summer flowering bulbs — even with compact spring and winter-flowering shrubs.

The bulbs may be planted beneath some shallow-rooted perennials. They will be in bloom during late winter, when most of the perennials are breaking their dormant period, and will have finished flowering by the time the earliest perennials reach blooming size. The summer-blooming bulbs will be ready to take over in turn, when these early perennials are fading. In the first year or two, you can cover your errors with a few patches of annuals to fill bare spots at unexpected times — but don't make it a habit!

PLANTING THE BORDER

Planting a border with perennials is certainly more expensive than doing it with annuals, but you must take the long-range view: once it's done, it's done for ever. There's no harm in passing the word around among gardening friends that you're planning a border — almost everyone has at least one overgrown clump that needs dividing!

Your planting is best carried out in late autumn, when most perennials are dormant and cut back. This is when you can best move them from other parts of your garden and take advantage of the kind offers of friends.

Most perennials can of course be raised economically from seed or cuttings, but this is a very slow way to start a border. Better buy as many plants or divisions as you can afford from your nurseryman. He may only stock a limited number of perennial species, but can order others for you with a little notice. Better still, order them yourself. You can have a great deal of fun during the autumn and winter by ordering from specialist nurserymen's advertisements in regular garden magazines.

As you have a lot of planting ahead of you, best order them to arrive staggered for several weekends' work. Start with the taller, or back plants, if you can.

When the plants do arrive, they'll be in good condition. Heel them in immediately in a spare corner of the garden until you're ready to plant. Give them a good sprinkle of water every day or two, and they'll survive and even start to grow.

Transfer your paper plan to the prepared, raked bed with string and stakes, allowing space between individual groups of plants according to their width at full size. Make sure both the bed and your original plan are to a fixed scale, otherwise you may finish up without enough plants to fill the space.

For best effect, your border should look crowded. This will also help keep down

weeds. Never plant one specimen of a type, but always groups of at least three and preferably seven or more. This will ensure worthwhile patches of colour when each species is in bloom, and will also provide mutual support for the plants in any one group.

Plant a full clump at a time, working along the bed. With a small planting fork, make a hollow for each plant in the clump, large enough to spread the roots properly. This is best done by placing the crown of the plant on a small hump in the prepared hole and spreading the roots out and down. Replace the soil and firm the plant in with your boot. When you've finished planting any group, you'll have a very irregular soil surface indeed. Keep handy a container of potting mix so you can even out the hollows and provide an extra ration of food for every plant.

When you've planted as much of the border as you can manage in a weekend, fork the surface soil over lightly between clumps, and finally rake it flat. This is not merely to keep your planting tidy, but to prevent rainwater lodging in the hollows and forming a hard crust on the soil. Finally, give the entire area a good sprinkling of bone meal and water long and deeply with a fine spray. In a few weeks, your perennials will start to grow and spread at a great rate if you've done your soil preparation properly.

MAINTENANCE OF THE BORDER

When the plants have reached full size, they'll generally keep weeds down by themselves, but in the early stages of growth, fork the topsoil over regularly and lightly, removing any weeds.

As the plants grow, a little staking and support will be needed, but keep this at a minimum, as the effect you're after is one of loose informality and abundant bloom. Really tall plants will need a group of three or four stakes around them. These can be connected by garden twine to give the growing clump some support against wind. For lower plants, an economical method of support is a group of well-branched twigs. These will be quickly covered by the plants they're supporting, and will soon be quite unobtrusive. That's the ideal form for a border, because nobody can see beauty through a forest of stakes.

Dead-head regularly during the warmer months by removing spent flowers. This will encourage the plants to turn their energy into side shoots instead of seeds.

In most areas, late autumn will see the end of the season's display and is the time for major tidying up. Go right over the border with a sharp pair of secateurs and cut each group of herbaceous perennials right back to ground level. At the same time, cut back the shrubby perennials to a more compact shape and trim any evergreen perennials of dead flower stems. When all this debris has been consigned to the compost head, you'll be able to get at the spaces between the plants. Fork over lightly so you don't damage surface roots, remove all dead material which might rot, and spread a surface mulch of well-decayed compost mixed with packaged plant food all over the bed. Top with a sprinkling of snail bait.

In very cold areas, some of the more delicate plants will need the protection of a covering of sand or dry peat to prevent frost-bite on new shoots; but in the southern hemisphere, this would only apply in mountainous inland areas. Such protection can be removed once danger of frost is past and the soil between plants again forked over to break up any surface crust.

In earliest spring, scatter blood and bone around the plants, sprinkle with the hose and the whole cycle is on its way for another year.

DIVIDING THE PLANTS
This is a tiresome but necessary chore if the plants are to stay vigorous. Fortunately, it only has to be done every fourth or fifth year. If you keep notes, you can stagger the work and do part of the border only in any one year.

All plants in each group must be dug up, split into smaller sections and replanted after the soil has been thoroughly turned over and enriched for the next few years. This applies to herbaceous perennials, but not to the shrubby types which have merely grown in size without increasing in numbers. Division is carried out during the dormant period, except for most of the daisies, which are usually divided in spring.

As you dig each clump, shake out the excess soil and reveal as much as possible of the root mass. Notice that the original pieces you planted have died out altogether, and that the healthiest-looking parts of the plant are toward the outside. These are the pieces you're after.

Some perennials, of course, don't like to be disturbed at all; these are noted in individual entries of the text.

In the case of many big plant clumps, the best technique is just to chop through with a spade, pull off any severed roots or dead stems and replant the sections at the same distance from each other as were the original plants. They'll soon recover from the vandalism.

Smaller plants of the surface-rooting type can often be pulled apart with two small planting forks back to back. Stick in the forks and lever them apart. Many *Primulas*, the smaller *Campanulas* and Shasta daisies can be pulled apart with the hands, or at worst with a sharp knife.

Whichever method of division you use, be particularly careful to remove all roots and bulbils of weeds before replanting, because it's the only opportunity you'll get for years. This is best done by hosing all the soil away from the root masses, when you'll be able to make out the intruders and pick them away.

You're bound to finish up with more plants than you need after this division, so the choice is yours. Either use them to replace groups that haven't done so well in your area, or give them away to friends. You won't have any shortage of takers among visitors who've seen your perennial border in full summer display!

How to use this book

All perennial plants for bed and border included in this book are arranged in the alphabetical order of their botanical names, so you can just leaf through until you come to the plant you want. If you know only a popular name, e.g., Leopard's Bane, turn to the comprehensive index beginning page 156. Here, each popular name will refer you to the plant's botanical name, and the number of the page on which the entry begins: e.g. Leopard's Bane, see *Doronicum* 62.

There are more popular names listed than there are entries in the book because many plants have more than one popular name.

Altogether, 309 species of perennial flowers are described, together with innumerable varieties. Over 260 are illustrated in colour. Each entry includes a great deal of useful information, some of it in abbreviated form in the heading. The first line of each entry gives the plant's generic name only, in large capital letters. This may be followed by a synonym (when there is one by which the plant is sometimes sold), e.g.,

AURINIA (syn ALYSSUM saxatile)
The Latin name is followed by one or more popular names in normal type. After this come three lines in heavy type, each prefixed by an asterisk. The first, e.g.,

*Summer-autumn
indicates the season in which the flower blooms. The second line, e.g.,

* Fast/long blooming
indicates first the plant's speed of growth to flowering size and following the oblique stroke the length of blooming season, generally short or long, sometimes all year. The third line, e.g.,

* Ht: to 150cm/5ft
indicates the plant's maximum height under ideal growing conditions and will help you decide where to plant. It will also suggest whether the plant may need staking — as in fact almost any perennial plant over 75cm/2½ft tall will, particularly in an exposed position. Sometimes, where several species are covered in the one entry, the height will be expressed in the form of a range, e.g.,

* Ht: 60-180cm/2-6ft

In such cases, comparative heights of individual species will be described in the entry itself. This line may also include an additional word e.g., **rampant, spreading,** when the plant's growth is exceptional in some way.

Finally, each heading includes a group of symbols, one or more in the form of a rayed sun, others as letters enclosed by squares.

☼ indicates the plant does best in full sun. These are ideal for open bedding.

◑ shows the plant prefers sun for only part of a day. These plants are ideal on the east or west side of your house.

● (the rarest) shows that the plant will flower in full shade. These would be ideal for use amongst trees.

[C] shows that the plant blooms well in cold-winter areas (though it may also grow elsewhere).

[T] that it flowers in any temperate climate (though its range may be much wider).

[H] that the plant does well in a hot climate (tropical to sub-tropical). Very few cold-climate plants will bloom in the sub-tropics as well.

As some plants are quite adaptable, however, the symbols may appear in many different combinations, as where a plant will grow in both cold and temperate climates, will bloom in full sun or part shade.

Information within the entry itself tells when to divide or grow from seed or plant out; time elapsed from seed sowing to blooming; correct spacing for good display and healthy growth (this will give you a clear idea of the plant's maximum width). You will also find the necessary temperatures and time for germination (appearance of the first leaves). There are descriptions of popular colour varieties, often with the names of commercially available strains. You will learn which flowers are fragrant, whether they should be sown in flats or in the open garden, the type of soil preferred, hints on watering, feeding, pruning and cutting back. Though each entry is necessarily brief, you'll find everything you need to know for planning and growing a dazzling display of colourful perennial flowers that will light up your garden year after year.

ACANTHUS spinosissimus
Spiny Acanthus

ACANTHUS mollis
Oyster Plant

ACANTHUS

Oyster Plant, Bear's Breech
* **Spring – summer**
* **Fast/long display**
* **Ht: 1.5m/4½ft**

Immortalized by the Greeks in the carved capitals of Corinthian columns, **Acanthus** species are grown mostly for their handsome foliage. Use them as a striking feature plant in semi-shade or the sheltered courtyard — but lay plenty of snail bait! Grow from autumn divisions or spring-sown seed at a temperature of 14°C/57°F. Germination takes about 3 weeks. Soil should be rich, well-drained and neutral in acidity. The satiny leaves vary greatly according to species, but are elegantly lobed and broadly toothed. Early summer flowers of mauve and grey appear in spikes up to 2m tall, after which the plant dies back. Slow to establish, **Acanthus** spreads rapidly when settled in. Dead-head after blooming and water generously except when dormant.

ACHILLEA filipendulina
Yarrow, Goldplate

ACHILLEA millefolium
Milfoil

ACHILLEA

Milfoil, Yarrow
* **Summer**
* **Fast/long blooming**
* **Ht: 50-150cm/20-60in**

☼ C T

Among the most trouble-free of perennials, the popular Yarrows (**Achillea** spp.) do well in any moderately fertile soil so long as it is fast draining. They may be propagated from winter divisions or from seed, which germinates in days if scattered lightly on the surface of a moist seed-raising mix and held at a temperature of about 21°C/70°F. Plant at 30-60cm intervals and water lightly. They are fairly drought-resistant, produce masses of dull, fern-like foliage with minimum water. Several bloomings can be expected each summer when you cut flower stems. **A. filipendulina** produces flat heads of tiny gold flowers, **A. millefolium** is deep pink, centred white. **A. ptarmica** (Sneezeweed) blooms greenish-white. All species should be cut back almost to ground level in winter, given complete fertilizer in spring.

17

ACONITUM vulparia
Wolfbane

ACONITUM napellus
Garden Monkshood

ACONITUM

Monkshood, Wolfbane
* **Summer**
* **Fast/long blooming**
* **Ht: 60-150cm/2-5ft**

Steeped in medieval mysticism, as their popular names suggest, there really is something sinister about these European perennials — they are poisonous in every part, were used in many potions of bygone days. Mostly they are tall-growing plants with helmet-shaped blue, purple or white flowers in late summer. Plant them 30-45cm apart in semi-shaded, rich soil. They grow easily from divisions or seed — but the latter may take 3 years to bloom after spring sowing at a temperature of 16°C/59°F. The deeply divided leaves are dark, satiny green, the flowers borne in tall racemes, often branched. **Aconitum napellus** blooms in violet-blue; **A. vulparia** may be mauve, pinkish or yellow. All die down in winter.

ACTINOTUS helianthi
Flannel Flower

ACTINOTUS

Flannel Flower
* **Spring – summer**
* **Average / long blooming**
* **Ht: 50cm-18in**

A curiosity of the Sydney sandstone region of New South Wales, the pale, furry Flannel Flower, **Actinotus helianthi** has become popular in gardens of Australian native plants, and is grown in other warm, dryish places such as southern California. It can also be used in cold-winter areas if treated as an annual. A sparse, erect-growing plant, it bears much-divided foliage of soft, greyish-green. In spring and summer, furry flowering stems of the same colour appear, each topped by one or more star-shaped inflorescences which may be 10cm wide. These consist of a composite mass of pink-stamened, greenish florets, the whole surrounded by generally 10-12 green-tipped, flannel-textured bracts of dull white. Like most Australian natives, they prefer good drainage and minimum disturbance. Plant in sandy, acid soil with a little humus and gravel. Propagate from divisions, cuttings or seed, which must be sown as soon as it is ripe and can take up to a year to germinate. Good for seaside or hot, dry areas, its needs are minimal once established.

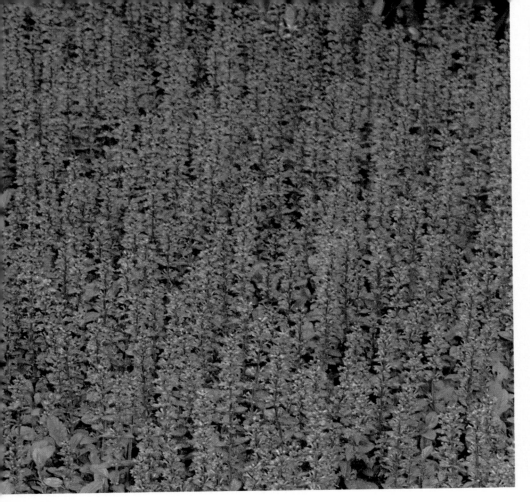

AJUGA reptans
Carpet Bugle

AJUGA

Bugleweed, Carpet Bugleweed
* **Spring – summer**
* **Fast/long blooming**
* **10-30cm/4-12in/spreading** C T

Colourful dwarf perennials mostly from Europe and Asia, the many attractive species of **Ajuga** spread rapidly from runners, are used to carpet the ground anywhere. They invariably look and grow better in shade. The Carpet or Blue Bugle, **A. reptans,** is the popular species, with neat rosettes of shining, elliptical leaves to 10cm in length. These may be deep green, bronze, purple, dark red or variegated with white and yellow. 'Burgundy Lace' is a showy multi-coloured variety. Propagate all varieties from division at any time, separating new plants and shortening their leaves before replanting at 20-30cm spacing for rapid cover. They enjoy well-drained, humus-rich soil and need regular water. A sprinkling of complete fertilizer at the rate of 200g to the square metre in early spring will ensure a heavy crop of warm-weather flowers. These appear in dense spikes and are generally a rich blue-violet, but paler blue, white, pink and purple-red cultivars are sometimes sold. Remove spent flowerheads and watch for fungus disease if drainage and air circulation are poor. Check this with a systemic fungicide.

ALCHEMILLA

Lady's Mantle
* **Summer**
*Fast/long display ☼ ☀ C T
* **Ht: 30-40cm /12-18in /spreading**

A member of the rose family (though you'd be hard put to spot the relationship) old-fashioned Lady's Mantle (**Alchemilla mollis**) is a delightful herbaceous perennial for moist, well-drained soil in a position with shade for at least part of the day. It can be raised from seed, sown under cover in early spring. The resultant seedlings are set out in autumn for bloom the following summer. Mature plants are generous in their produc-tion of new seedlings — or can be divided any time between autumn and spring and set out at 45cm intervals. **Alchemilla** is bushy in habit, producing masses of pale green, palmate leaves that have rounded lobes and lightly-toothed edges. These somewhat resemble those of a **Pelargonium** and are covered in woolly hairs. The dainty yellow-green flowers are without petals and scarcely larger than a pin's head. They appear in dense trusses throughout summer, turning the entire planting into a mass of gold. Plants should be kept continuously moist. They are cut back to about 3cm above ground when blooming is done.

ALCHEMILLA mollis
Lady's Mantle

ANAPHALIS

Pearl or Pearly Everlasting
* **Summer**
* **Fast/long display**
* **Ht: 30-100cm/1-3ft**

Bearing a strong resemblance to southern-hemisphere **Helichrysums,** the 30-odd species of **Anaphalis** are found on all continents north of the equator. They are members of the daisy family, greatly valued in the mixed border for their heads of small, silvery daisy flowers and can be cut and dried for long-lasting arrangements. Easy to grow, they can be propagated in many different ways: from 7.5cm spring cuttings; from divisions of the plant taken in autumn or early spring; and from seed which may be sown under cover in winter, and will germinate in about two weeks at a temperature of 13-18°C/44-64°F. The young plants are set out in spring at spacings of 45cm and spread quickly into a mass of long, pointed leaves, generally a woolly grey-green on their reverse side. The flowers appear in many-branched umbels, yellow centres surrounded by a mass of papery white bracts. They prefer an alkaline soil with only moderate water, and are quite drought-resistant. Divide and replant every 3 or 4 years. Prune hard in autumn.

ANAPHALIS margaritacea
Pearly Everlasting

ANEMONE nemorosa
Wood Anemone

ANEMONE

Windflower, Lily-of-the-Field
* **Spring – autumn**
* **Average /short blooming**
* **15-150cm /6-36in**

C T

This spectacular genus of garden flowers takes its most popular common name from the fragility of individual blooms, which are inclined to shatter and blow away after a few days. There are well over 100 species from cool-temperate areas of the northern hemisphere, but they are commonly represented in gardens only by the garish spring-flowering type which is mostly treated as an annual and bracketed with **Ranunculus,** which belong to the same family. The most spectacular **Anemone** varieties for the perennial border are a hyb-

rid group of Japanese and Chinese species which are mostly autumn-blooming. These are generally taller plants and include as one parent either the pink-flowered **A. hupehensis** or the white-blooming **A. vitifolia** (Grape-leaf Anemone). These hybrids are generally planted out from divisions at spacings of 30-60cm in colder weather. They enjoy sheltered semi-shade in soil that is both well-drained and water-retentive. They resent distubance and will make little growth the first year, but once established, spread into a dense clump and reward you regularly with flowering stems 75-100cm in height, year after year. Entire stems should be cut as they fade, and the whole plant cut back to ground level when blooming has finished. A good ration of complete fertilizer in early spring, followed by light cultivation, will start the blooming

ANEMONE X *lesseri*
Spring Windflower

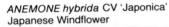

ANEMONE hybrida CV 'Japonica'
Japanese Windflower

ANEMONE X 'Lorelei'
Chinese Windflower

ANEMONE (continued)

cycle all over again. White-flowered **A. hybrida** var. **alba** (also known as **A. japonica**) is the tallest, sometimes reaching 150cm. Delicate pink **A.** x 'Lorelei' generally peaks at 1m. Both have handsome, trifoliate leaves, mid-green and slightly hairy. Variety x **lesseri** has white-centred crimson flowers and foliage divided like a buttercup's. It is a smaller plant, rarely reaching 45cm, and should be planted out at 30cm spacings. It is particularly effective in shaded rock gardens and blooms early summer. All can be multiplied from root cuttings or from seed, which is sown outdoors in late autumn for germination the following spring. The illustrated European Wood Anemone (**A. nemorosa**) is a dainty spring-flowering species often used for naturalizing under trees. It grows from root divisions. The trifoliate leaves are deeply divided, and the delicate 7-petalled flowers may be pink, white or powder blue according to variety. It rarely passes 20cm in height; individual blooms being only 2.5cm in diameter, but borne in profusion.

24

ANTHEMIS tinctoria
Golden Marguerite

ANTHEMIS

Golden Marguerite, Ox-eye Chamomile
* **Summer – autumn**
* **Fast /all season**
* **Ht: 60-100cm /2-3ft**

☼ C T

Most brilliant of the summer-flowering daisies, the golden Ox-eye Chamomile **(Anthemis tinctoria)** shines blindingly right through to autumn, and makes a dazzling display in the summer border, when allowed to sprawl in a haphazard fashion. Their dense, fern-like foliage is attractive all year, and highly aromatic when crushed. It is a source of chamomile tea. The 5cm daisy-flowers are bright yellow, open individually on 60-100cm stems. They pick well, and have been used for centuries as the source of a yellow dye. Plant them out in well-drained soil, spacing the plants about 35cm apart. Fertilize with a light hand and give occasional water. The flower display lasts for months and will be prolonged by cutting back the spent stems after flowers fade. Though perennial, the plants are not long-lasting and should be renewed every second year, either from cuttings or from seed which can be sown in winter under cover at a temperature of 21°C/70°F. Germination will take about two weeks. Also grown is the dwarf **A. cupaniana** with silvery-grey, fern-like foliage and white summer flowers and **A. sancti-johanni** (the Bulgarian Chamomile) which has deeply-lobed, softly-pubescent greyish leaves and bright orange daisy blooms. It grows to 45cm.

AQUILEGIA CV 'Biedermeier'
Columbine

AQUILEGIA CV 'Nora Barlow'
Double Columbine

AQUILEGIA

Columbine, Granny's Bonnets
* **Spring – summer**
* **Fast/long season** ☼ ☀ C T
* **Ht: 25-60cm/10-24in**

Given semi-shade and alkaline soil in a position that never dries out — you can grow old-fashioned Columbines to perfection! Leaves like lacy maidenhair fern and long-spurred flowers in a range of rich colours give a cool, woodland effect all through the warmer months. Set nursery-bought plants out in autumn, or sow summer seed which will take about a month to germinate. Leave the seeds uncovered on a moistened seed-raising mix. Illustrated hybrids are low-growing 'Beidermeier' in a wide range of colours, and 'Nora Barlow', a spurless double cultivar of **Aquilegia vulgaris.** Plants are relatively short-lived and should be replaced every 3 years. Cut flower stems to the ground after blooms, but leave a few pods for self-seeding.

ARABIS

Rock Cress
* **Winter – summer**
* **Fast /all season**
* **Ht: 22cm /9in /spreading**

☼ C T

Charming but unspectacular plants for the rock or alpine garden, or for crevices in steps, walls and paving, the perennial Rock Cresses form dense mats of grey-green leaf-rosettes and are often used to over-plant spring-flowering bulbs. Most commonly seen of more than 100 species is the ubiquitous **Arabis albida** (also known as **A. caucasica** and **A. alpina**). It is set out from divisions in autumn at a spacing of 40cm, but can also be grown from seed sown indoors at 21°C /**70°F** with the seeds left uncovered. **Arabis** likes sandy, well-drained soil and needs little water. It should be cut back hard when bloom is over. Like other members of the mustard family (Cruciferae) it is prone to fungus diseases and should be watched in humid weather. There are both white and pink-flowered varieties.

ARABIS albida 'Flore Pleno'
Double Rock Cress

ARMERIA maritima
Thrift, Sea Pink

ARMERIA

Thrift, Sea Pink
* **Spring – autumn**
* **Average /all season**
* **Ht: 12-30cm /5-12in**

☼ C T

Gay little evergreen perennials that look like grassy cushions all year, **Armerias** are mostly native to the Mediterranean and Asia Minor, where they are found in mountain meadows and along rocky coasts. They like gravelly, well-drained soil and need little water, though they appreciate an annual sprinkling of slow-release fertilizer. Provided spent flower stems are cut regularly, they'll keep up a constant display of pink, white or deep rose bloom from spring through to autumn. Propagate from winter division, summer cuttings, or in spring from well-soaked seed which will germinate in less than three weeks at a temperature of 18°C /64°F. Set plants out at 20-30cm spacings. Watch for rust disease in spring, spray with fungicide.

ARUNCUS sylvester
Goat's Beard

ARUNCUS

Goat's Beard

* **Summer**
* **Fast/short blooming season**
* **Ht: 1-2m/3-7ft/spreading**

A graceful woodland perennial that's at home in any semi-shaded location, quaintly named Goat's Beard grows rather too large for comfort and may best be set in a wild garden — though it also looks sensational by a pool or creek. Wherever, it demands deep, rich soil to give of its best, and roots should be kept moist at all times. **Aruncus sylvester** is a rose-relative and there is a distinct resemblance in its handsome pale green leaves, each with many finely-pleated, ovate leaflets. The flowers are another matter: tiny, white and borne in plume-like panicles high above the dense foliage. Cut flowering stems back hard in autumn, plant out from divisions in the same season.

ASCLEPIAS incarnata
Swamp Milkweed

ASCLEPIAS

Milkweed, Butterfly Weed
* **Summer**
* **Fast/long season**
* **Ht: 120cm/4ft**

A large genus of plants from the Americas and Africa, **Asclepias** are represented in gardens by two perennial species. The Blood Flower, **A. curassavica** is for warm climate gardens only, a woody plant with bright, crown-shaped orange and red flowers in umbels at the upper leaf axils. It is grown from spring-sown seed. North American **A. incarnata** or Swamp Milkweed is for cooler areas. It grows 60-120cm high from cold weather root divisions. Both like a deep, rich soil with leaf-mould and peat. Regular water and an annual spring feeding help them remain fresh and green. The narrow leaves of both species are similar, but **A. incarnata's** tiny flesh-pink flowers open from brick coloured buds. The name Milkweed refers to the sticky sap, so attractive to butterflies.

ASTER novi-belgii ▶
'Patricia Ballard'

28

ASTER novi-belgii
'Crimson Brocade'

ASTER novi-belgii
New York Aster

ASTER

Michaelmas or Easter Daisy
* **Summer – autumn**
* **Fast/long blooming**
* **Ht: 45-150cm/18-60in**

C T

Not the plant commonly called Aster or China Aster **(Callistephus chinensis),** the true **Asters** are a vast genus of 500 and more perennial plants, found on all continents except Australia. Though many have individual popular names, they are collectively known in the northern hemisphere as Michaelmas daisies, because their peak flowering is around the end of September — conversely, south of the equator they are called Easter Daisies. Whichever name you use they are, as a group, among the most rewarding of all herbaceous perennials, reliably sending up tall panicles of showy daisy flowers year after year. Many species and innumerable colour varieties are grown. The Italian Aster, **A. amellus,** grows to 60cm, has rough-textured greyish lanceolate leaves and blue-lilac flowers. North American **A. ericoides** or Heath Aster grows to 1m, bears many-branched stems of 1cm white or pinkish bloom, has very narrow leaves. **A. X frikartii** is a Eurasian hybrid of 75cm with dark, rough leaves and orange-centred violet-blue flowers, 5cm across. **A. linosyris** (found all around the Mediterranean and across to the Caucasus) is popularly known as Goldilocks. Its bright yellow flowers appear in late summer, right at stem tips, and it has narrow dull-green foliage. North American **A. novae-angliae** (the New England Aster) grows tallest, sometimes to 1.5m, and is available in many colour varieties with flowers from 2.5 to 5cm across. Its stem-clasping leaves are distinctive. **A. novi-belgii** (the New York Aster) is the parent of most commonly grown hybrids, in colour varieties of white, blue, mauve, pink, crimson and purple. Flowers are slightly larger than other species, leaves more narrowly pointed. Illustrated cultivars 'Patricia Ballard' and 'Crimson Brocade' are typical. All species are planted out from division of established clumps in late autumn — each division having young shoots surrounding an old stem, and ample roots. Set out low-growing varieties at 30cm intervals, taller growers from 45 to 60cm apart. **A.**

ASTER ericoides
Heath Aster

ASTER linosyris
Goldilocks

ASTER X frikartii
Hybrid Aster

ericoides and **A. novi-belgii** will probably need staking in early summer to prevent the stems flopping under their enormous burden of bloom. All **Aster** species prefer full sun, except in very hot areas, when they will gratefully accept a semi-shaded position. They thrive in any fertile soil, but it must be well-drained and preferably enriched with peat or leaf-mould. Plants should be kept moist at all times because of their massive growth, and benefit from a ration of complete fertilizer through spring and summer. This could be at a rate of 30g per plant. Clumps will need to be tidied up after blooming, when all flowering stems can be cut back to ground level. Most **Aster** species produce side shoots at a great rate, which is just as well, for they are generally short-lived and plants should be replaced every three years or so. All can be grown from seed, sown at any time with a germinating temperature of 21°C/70°F — but as they rarely come true to colour, you will probably prefer to propagate by division as noted above.

31

ASTILBE X 'Mont Blanc'
False Spiraea

ASTILBE X 'Rotlicht'
False Spiraea

ASTILBE

False Spiraea, Goat's Beard
* **Summer**
* **Fast/long blooming**
* **Ht: 60-200cm/2-6ft**

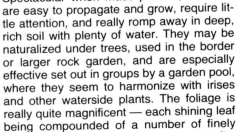

Spectacular when mass planted, **Astilbes** are easy to propagate and grow, require little attention, and really romp away in deep, rich soil with plenty of water. They may be naturalized under trees, used in the border or larger rock garden, and are especially effective set out in groups by a garden pool, where they seem to harmonize with irises and other waterside plants. The foliage is really quite magnificent — each shining leaf being compounded of a number of finely pleated leaflets. A rich green at maturity, they are often distinctly pink or copper-toned when young. The flowers appear in

32

1m tall, plume-like panicles in late spring and early summer, and are good for cutting. Each panicle, which may branch freely, consists of hundreds of tiny 4- and 5-petalled flowers coloured from white through every shade of pink to darkest red, according to variety. Most garden cultivars are grouped under the name **A. X arendsii** and are hybrids of the species **A. davidii** var. **chinensis** with various other Asian species. They vary in height from 60 to 100cm according to their particular parentage. **Astilbes** are replanted from divisions set 60cm apart in early spring, and should be shaded in warm weather until their roots are well established. They can also be grown from seed, which is sown indoors in winter at a temperature range of 16-21°C/ 60-70°F. If this can be maintained, germination should take about 28 days. The only other species much grown are **A. chinensis pumila,** a dwarf (22cm) rockery plant with erect panicles of rosy bloom, and the taller-growing **A. grandis** or Giant Spiraea which may reach 2m in height and should be planted at 60cm spacings. Its blooms are pure white but borne in spreading, showy panicles. It is a plant for the very large garden and hard to obtain. Recommended named cultivars of **A. X arendsii** include 'Deutschland' (60cm, white); 'Federsee' (75cm, rosy red); 'Mont Blanc' (100cm, white); 'Rhineland' (75cm, pink); 'Rotlicht' (60cm, dark red). **Astilbes** should be cut back to the ground in late autumn, lifted and divided every three years.

ASTILBE X *arendsii*
Hybrid Astilbes

ASTRANTIA *major*
Masterwort

ASTRANTIA *carniolica*
Balkan Masterwort

ASTRANTIA

Masterwort
* **Summer**
* **Slow/long display**
* **Ht: 60-100cm/2-3ft**

 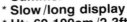

Several species of this small perennial genus (a division of the carrot family) have a great popularity with European gardeners. Native to Europe and the Near East, **Astrantias** grow well in any soil in part shade, but really sparkle in full sun so long as the soil is constantly moist. The attractive leaves are much divided and delicately pointed, the small starry flowers in subdued combinations of pink, white and green are arranged in many-branched umbels, each head surrounded by green bracts. **Astrantias** are propagated from divisions in late autumn to early spring. They can also be raised from seed sown early autumn, and the seedings planted out about 18 months later. Flowering stems are cut back in autumn.

AURINIA

(syn ALYSSUM saxatile)

Basket of Gold, Gold Dust, Yellow Alyssum, Mad Wort
* **Spring – summer**
* **Average /long display**
* **Ht: 20-30cm /long display**
* **Ht: 20-30cm /8-12in**

So many of us have known and loved the plant pictured below as Yellow Alyssum, it may come as a shock to learn it is in reality **Aurinia saxatilis**! But no name change can detract from its incredible beauty in the spring and early summer garden. Then, its neat mound of greyish leaf rosettes suddenly bursts into a blinding mass of tiny golden flowers, the display persisting for months. **Aurinia** is a woody-rooted, sub-shrubby sort of plant, evergreen and grown from cuttings or seed. The former are taken after bloom ends, inserted in a mixture of sand and peat and potted up when rooted, keeping them under glass through winter. They should be ready to set out at spacings of 30-45cm the following spring. Seed can be sown directly in the flowering position in spring, or indoors in winter, where it will germinate in about two weeks at a temperature of 13-24°C/55-75°F. The seed needs light to sprout and should merely be sprinkled on the surface. Shear the plant back hard when flowering is over, and seek out named colour varieties in every shade from cream to almost orange. The golden yellow, however, is most eye-catching.

AURINIA saxatilis
Basket of Gold

BEGONIA coccinea
Corazon de Jesus

BEGONIA argenteo-guttata
Trout-leaf Begonia

BEGONIA

Begonia
* **Spring – autumn**
* **Average /long display**
* **Ht: 60-180cm /2-6ft**

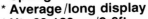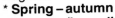

A large genus of perennial plants found in the sub-tropics of both hemispheres, most of the 1000-odd **Begonia** species can be grown in the open garden only in areas with temperate to sub-tropical climates. Their succulent stems and foliage are completely destroyed by frost, and northern hemisphere gardeners must be content to grow most of them in the greenhouse, or as indoor plants, with but a shadow of their tropical luxuriance. All **Begonias** are in fact perennial — though the ever-popular dwarf wax type **(B. semperflorens)** is frequently used as an annual. There are species that grow from tubers and rhizomes and these will be dealt with in a forthcoming volume devoted to those sorts of plants — but here we are concerned with the

36

fibrous-rooted species, sometimes referred to as 'cane-stemmed **Begonias**'. Most of these are from South America and prefer a light, sandy soil enriched with peat and leaf-mould. They are grown in full or semi-shade and need continual water. They can be grown from seed, which is very fine and should be left uncovered by soil on top of a moist seed-raising mix at temperatures between 21-24°C/70-75°F. More commonly, they are propagated from divisions or cuttings, which are taken just below a stem node and can be rooted in water in a bright window. All of these cane-stemmed **Begonias** flower, mostly with small, satiny four-petalled blooms in colourfully-stemmed panicles. But their great glory is in their foliage, which is formed in a wide range of shapes (mostly asymmetrical and ear-shaped) and in a wide range of colours, often exotically marked with contrasting spots and streaks. Most species must be watched for fungus diseases such as grey mould and powdery mildew, and of course snails find the succulent foliage irresistible. Older plants can be tidied up by cutting out 2 or 3-year-old flowered stems. A dose of liquid fertilizer in early spring will stimulate new growth, and regular water in hot weather is essential. Illustrated varieties are typical.

BEGONIA scharfii
Elephant-ear Begonia

BERGENIA cordifolia
Megasea, Saxifraga

BERGENIA

Heartleaf, Saxifraga, Megasea
* **Winter – spring**
* **Average/long blooming**
* **Ht: 30cm/12in/spreading**

Useful for winter cut flowers in a mild climate, **Bergenia** blooms a little later where the climate is hard, as in its native Siberia. It grows easily in almost any soil, provided it is enriched with leaf mould and receives plenty of water in hot weather. But you'll see these handsome plants at their best in damp, woodsy soil in semi-shade. There they make splendid ground cover with their great, leath-

ery, toothed leaves up to 25cm in diameter. The fleshy flower stems (usually drooping) may reach 40cm in length and bear massive panicles of 2.5cm pink to lilac flowers with a charming perfume — that is, they do if you remember to protect them against marauding slugs and snails! **Bergenias** can be propagated from rooted divisions from autumn to spring, or from seed which may be sown outdoors in autumn for spring germination. If you're in a hurry, sow them indoors at a temperature of 13°C/55°F, when germination can be expected in about three weeks. They grow into dense clumps, and should be divided every few years. Spent flower heads should be removed.

BRUNNERA

Siberian Bugloss
* **Spring – summer**
* **Fast/long display** ☼ ☀ C T
* **Ht: 30-45cm /12-18in**

Found all over the vast reaches of the Russian Steppes from Siberia to the Caucasus, hardy **Brunnera macrophylla** is a favourite herbaceous perennial for planting in large drifts or naturalizing under trees. Its general appearance is that of a large forget-me-not with heart-shaped leaves — and in fact it is sometimes listed as **Anchusa myosotidiflora** in token of its pale blue flowers which appear in 50cm arching sprays. **Brunneras** will thrive in any ordinary garden soil, and in almost any position, even full sun if you can keep up the water in summer. They are at their best, however, in leafy soil or semi-shade. Propagate them from division of the root mass any time between late autumn and early spring — spacing the new plantings at 45cm intervals. To multiply your stock of plants, take root cuttings in autumn, set them in a mix of sand and peat in equal parts and keep them under glass. They should be ready to plant out late the following spring when new leaves are developing, but won't mature fully until the autumn. This process will probably prove unnecessary as the plants, once established, self-seed readily. As with most herbaceous perennials, flowering stems should be cut as they fade, leaving a few for seeding. **B. macrophylla** has an attractive variety with cream-variegated leaves, which is most striking in a shaded position. As with the plain-leaf variety, these are rough-textured, heart-shaped and prominently veined — somewhat resembling the leaves of a violet.

BRUNNERA *macrophylla*
Siberian Bugloss

39

CALCEOLARIA integrifolia
Slipper Flower

CALCEOLARIA

Slipper Flower, Pocketbook Plant
* **Summer**
* **Slow/long-blooming**
* **Ht: 45-180cm/1½-6ft**

An evergreen, sub-shrubby perennial from Chile, this larger version of the popular annual flowering pot plant is a more attractive and versatile subject in almost every way, though without the latter's wide colour range. For one thing, it can be grown out-of-doors in a wide range of climates. It enjoys heat, and although not completely frost hardy, **Calceolaria integrifolia** will generally survive with a minimum of damage. It can be grown indoors in a pot or hanging basket; or in the open garden, where it enjoys crowding and prefers an acid, moderately rich soil with only occasional watering. Grow from spring-sown seed which will germinate in 5-10 days at a temperature range of 13-21°C/55-70°F. Seedlings are planted in their final position when well grown. Propagation from hardened wood cuttings is also practised. The 7.5cm lanceolate leaves are matte-textured and finely wrinkled; the golden-yellow flowers are less than 2cm in diameter with a heavily pouched lower lip. They are borne in irregular cymes throughout the summer. Trim to a more manageable shape in autumn.

CALLISIA

(syn SPIRONEMA, RECTANTHERA)

Inch Plant
* **Summer**
* **Fast/long display**
* **Ht: 60cm/2ft/spreading**

An interesting perennial for warmer-climate gardens, the showy Inch Plant, **Callisia fragrans,** spread far and fast, and is basically a larger, more spectacular Wandering Jew or Spiderwort. Grow it at the front of the border, or as a splashy groundcover; it is easy to propagate from rooted sections of the long, running stems. Each will grow up to 60cm tall in any soil, and with moderate water will send out further runners clothed with long, waxy leaves 30cm in length. These taper to a rosette, from which long, red-stemmed flower panicles develop in summer. Each consists of clusters of tiny, white, fragrant flowers that wilt soon after opening in full sun. The plant is colourful year round, with a proportion of the leaves showing red or purple.

CALLISIA fragrans
Inch Plant

CALTHA palustris
Kingcup

CALTHA

Kingcup, Marsh Marigold
* **Spring**
* **Fast/long display**
* **Ht: 30-60cm/12-24in**

What a collection of popular names this showy perennial has totted up! Kingcup, May-blob, Meadow-bright, Marsh Marigold — but the first describes **Caltha palustris** best, for what is it but a king-sized buttercup? A hardy, herbaceous perennial that grows wonderfully by the margin of a pool, in boggy soil — even right in the water if it's not too deep — it sends up masses of hollow-stemmed, handsome rounded leaves, each up to 18cm wide and lightly toothed. These are joined in late spring by 60cm stems of generally golden-yellow cup-shaped flowers (though there are paler varieties). **Caltha** produces plenty of seeds and seedlings, but may also be propagated by division of the roots soon after flowers fade. Rust may be a problem, is treated with a fungicide.

41

CAMPANULA X *latiloba*
'Hidcote Lavender'

CAMPANULA

Bellflower
* **Summer – autumn**
* **Average/long display**
* **15-150cm/6-60in**

A popular genus of more than 250 species, the **Campanulas** or bellflowers mostly originate from the wild in Europe, and have been hybridized to produce an enormous range of useful garden plants for the rockery, border, wild garden or even hanging baskets. All of the popular species except one are perennial, and though their blooms vary greatly in size, shape and height of inflorescence, all provide a welcome range of blue tones for every garden use. They may be propagated from seed sown out-of-doors in late spring or summer for the following year's display, or sown indoors at a constant temperature range of 20-30°C/68-86°F. Germination time varies from 14-21 days according to species. Perennial types may also be propagated by division of the clumps or from stem cuttings of firmer wood struck under glass in a mixture of sand and peat. Plants should be set out at spacings of between 10 and 45cm according to the ultimate size of the species concerned. All enjoy a rich, well-drained soil that is kept constantly moist, and most perform best in full sun. But the Harebell and Peach-leaf Bellflowers are also useful in part shade, where colours remain brighter. Of the illustrated species, **C. lac-**

CAMPANULA rotundifolia
Harebell

CAMPANULA isophylla
Star of Bethlehem

CAMPANULA carpatica
Tussock Bellflower

CAMPANULA latifolia 'Alba'
Giant Bellflower

CAMPANULA lactiflora
'Milky Bellflower'

CAMPANULA persicifolia
Peach-leaf Bellflower

CAMPANULA (continued)

tiflora and **C. latifolia** are tall-growing plants, sending up their stems of open, bell-shaped blooms in dense terminal panicles to a height of 2m. **C. latiloba** and **C. persicifolia** (the latter with more cup-shaped blooms on unbranched stems, and leaves in a dense, basal rosette) are satisfied to reach 1m in height, and are decorative toward the front of the border. **C. carpatica** and **C. rotundifolia** are popular for rock garden work where they rarely pass 30cm in height but form dense clumps. Finally, the Star of Bethlehem or Italian Bellflower **(C. isophylla)** is most commonly seen as a hanging-basket plant in both white and blue flower forms. It reaches only 15cm inheight but may trail 45cm in every direction. It is not so frost-hardy as the other species, which are generally cut back to the ground in autumn. Taller-growing **Campanula** species should be divided each 3-4 years or whenever they show signs of overcrowding.

CENTAUREA

Knapweed, Centaury
* **Summer – autumn**
* **Average/long display**
* **Ht: 45-150cm/18-60in**

☼ C T

Native to Europe and the Middle East, the **Centaureas** have been grown since ancient times and may have been used in medicine, since one of them, the illustrated Globe Centaury, is said to have healed a wound in the foot of Chiron, the wisest of all the centaurs and mentor of Hercules. Though the annual Bachelor Button (**C. cyanus**) is best known of the group, several hundred other species are known and grown. They mostly prefer a neutral, well-drained soil and perennial species can be propagated by division or by seed, which is sown in spring and summer for bloom the following year. Leaves are generally silky-hairy, those of **C. dealbata** being deeply divided. The showy daisy-type blooms come in many colours, in the case of yellow **C. macrocephala** are borne on stems up to 1.5m in height.

CENTAUREA macrocephala
Globe Centaury

CENTAUREA dealbata
Persian Knapweed

CEPHALARIA gigantea
Tatar Pincushion

CHEIRANTHUS mutabilis variegatus
Moroccan Wallflower

CEPHALARIA

Tatar Pincushion
* **Summer**
* **Average /long blooming**
* **Ht: 2m /6ft**

Looking at the many beautiful plants that come from Siberia, we may spare a thought for the many Russian scientists who've spent long, involuntary vacations there. The Giant or Tatar Pincushion **(Cephalaria gigantea (syn C. tatarica))** is one of these plants, a beautiful 2m herbaceous perennial for the larger border or as a naturalized subject. It will grow in any soil, is naturally frost-hardy, and resembles a large yellow scabious, to which it is related. Grow it from autumn divisions or from seed, which germinates under cover at a temperature of 21-24°C/70-75°F. Plants are set out at 45cm spacings and will certainly need light staking as they grow beyond the 1m mark. Dead-head regularly to prolong bloom and cut back in late autumn.

CHEIRANTHUS

Perennial Wallflower
* **Spring – summer**
* **Average /long blooming**
* **Ht: 30cm /12in**

This hardy, sub-shrubby perennial version of the common wallflower has little in common with English cottage gardens but comes from exotic Morocco! Firstly its flowers are a delectable mauve-pink rather than the ruddy oranges and yellows of the English species. Secondly, they have beautifully variegated foliage — grey-green margined with cream. Thirdly, they have less perfume. **Cheiranthus mutabilis variegatus** is the name, and it will grow well in almost any soil that is between neutral and alkaline. It is grown from woody cuttings or from seed. Sowing should take place in spring or late summer, maintaining a temperature of 13-19°C/55-65°F until the seedlings appear in about a week. An economical watering in the growing season is its only real need, but occasional fertilization will certainly pay off.

CHRYSANTHEMUM X 'Morning Star'
Charm Chrysanthemum

CHRYSANTHEMUM

Chrysanthemum , Marguerite,
Pyrethrum, Shasta Daisy, etc.
* **Spring – autumn**
* **Variable / long blooming**
* **Ht: 30-120cm / 12-48in** C T

Chrysanthemums may not be the largest genus of perennial plants, but at times they seem like it due to their profusion of colour, shape and size. In fact there are probably fewer than 150 natural species in the whole world, but they have been so crossed, hybridized, irradiated and improved that nobody could keep track of all the named varieties. I will merely attempt to whet your appetite with a few of the more common and interesting species available. In alphabetical order these are: **C. coccineum,** the Painted Daisy or Persian Insect Flower — this is a slender, usually unbranched plant of 60cm, pale fernlike foliage and 7.5cm daisy flowers that may vary from palest pink to the glowing crimson of our illustration. It is raised from seed sown outdoors in summer, or indoors at a temperature of 21°C/70°F. Germination takes about a month. A popular cut flower, it is also raised commercially as the source of Pyrethrum insecticides. Plant 30cm apart in rich, well-drained soil. **C. frutescens** is the Paris Daisy or Marguerite, a bushy, woody-based plant introduced from the Canary Islands in the 16th century. It was named for Queen Marguerite de Valois, in whose Paris garden it grew before 1600. They *can* be grown from seed but the preferred method is cuttings. Just take 20cm slips, strip the lower leaves and plant. With regular pinching out they'll become a flowering-size bush in no time. Many colour varieties are available, both single and double. **C.** X **morifolium** is the Florist's Chrysanthemum

CHRYSANTHEMUM X *superbum*
Shasta Daisy

CHRYSANTHEMUM *coccineum*
Pyrethrum, Painted Daisy

CHRYSANTHEMUM *frutescens*
Marguerite Daisy

CHRYSANTHEMUM (continued)

or 'Mum' in its myriad varieties. These are mostly complicated hybrids between the natural Asian species **C. indicum, C. japanense, C. makinoi, C. ornatum** and many others. They have been improved over thousands of years by the Japanese, whose national flower they have become. They do best in a rich, well-drained soil, which is often manured by professional growers, and their peak bloom is late autumn, triggered by the lengthening night hours. Potted specimens sold in bloom at other times of the year are forced by raising them in greenhouses which can be artificially darkened. The Florist's Chrysanthemums can be grown from seed, but the preferred method is from cuttings of basal shoots taken in early spring or from division of established clumps. At the outset, you must decide whether you want quwlity or quantity. Giant exhibition 'Mums' like the illustrated 'Frances Jefferson' are produced by removing all but a single bud and fertilized heavily so the plant's growing energy goes into producing a single, gigantic flower which may be 22.5cm in diameter. This is usually done under cover with maximum protection from the weather. These giant ornamental **Chrysanthemums** are available in a wide variety of bloom styles — the Quilled or Spider Chrysanthemums like 'Yellow Nightingale' being the most startling. Dwarf-growing Charm varieties like 'Morning Star' are stimulated to produce many small blooms by constant pinching back. Finally in our limited repertoire, we cannot overlook the ever-popular Shasta Daisy, **C. superbum** (syn **C. maximum**). This too is a hybrid of several European species, grows to 120cm and is a favourite cut flower. Though always white, it has many flower varieties, single and double, some with fringed petals. Shastas have dark, shiny, toothed leaves in dense basal rosettes and send up their flowers singly on tall stems during warm weather. They too are propagated by division of clumps in early spring. All **Chrysanthemums** must be dead-headed for prolonged bloom, and growing flower buds should be sprayed regularly to forestall caterpillar destruction.

CHRYSANTHEMUM X 'Frances Jefferson'
Exhibition Chrysanthemum
CHRYSANTHEMUM X 'Yellow Nightingale'
Fantasy Chrysanthemum

CLEMATIS integrifolia
Virgin's Bower

CLEMATIS

Virgin's Bower, Leather Flower
* **Summer**
* **Fast/long blooming**
* **Ht: 1m/3ft**

Though the vast majority of 200 **Clematis** species are beautiful climbing plants, there are at least a dozen others which do not climb and can be truly classified as herbaceous perennials for the bed or border. These other **Clematis,** often with smaller, more subtle blooms and interesting foliage, rarely grow taller than 120cm. They are members of the ranunculus family, and flourish in neutral to alkaline soil that is well-drained and thoroughly enriched with leafmould before planting takes place in the colder months. Like the climbing species, these herbaceous **Clematis** need their roots in a cool, moist, shaded position, say on the shaded side of a smaller shrub or evergreen perennial. There, with minimum support, they will rapidly rise to their full height over the spring months. They are grown from divisions or 7.5cm basal cuttings taken in spring and rooted under glass in a mixture of peat and sand. These should be ready for planting out in autumn. Herbaceous **Clematis** do not appreciate cultivation around the root area. They do, however, benefit from a deep summer mulch, and are cut back to ground level in winter. Illustrated **C. integrifolia** is inclined to be weak-stemmed and so requires more support than some others. This may take the form of one or more 1m stakes, or a chickenwire cylinder of similar height to which they can be tied. Feed at monthly intervals during the growing season.

COREOPSIS

Tickseed, Calliopsis
* **Spring – autumn**
* **Fast/long season**
* **Ht: 45-90cm /18-36in**

☼ T

Coreopsis are so easy to grow, details of any sort should be unnecessary. Perennial, golden-flowered **C. lanceolata** has become naturalized all over the world, and might be considered a pest if it were not so beautiful. It grows from a rosette of simple, slender, dark green leaves, and self-sows freely. Related **C. verticillata** has leaves that are similar, but divided, and more regularly-shaped blooms. It is propagated from autumn and spring division, each division having several shoots. It should be re-planted at 45cm intervals in rich, well-drained soil and dead-headed regularly for continuous bloom. **Coreopsis** are drought resistant, need water only when flopped.

COREOPSIS verticillata
Tickseed

COREOPSIS lanceolata
Calliopsis

CORYDALIS

Corydalis
* **Spring – autumn**
* **Average/long blooming**
* **Ht: 40cm/15in**

How strange that these delicate-looking relatives of the poppies have never acquired a general common name. They are certainly one of the most widespread of perennial genera (over 300 species of them found in the northern hemisphere and South Africa) and they can be planted almost anywhere with a rich, damp soil that is also well drained. Growing them in wall crevices is one popular technique — getting them to stop is rather more of a problem, for they self-seed with abandon. Be sure to root out excess plants to keep them within bounds. If you don't have them already, sow seed where you want them in late winter. Charming **Corydalis lutea** has dainty maidenhair foliage, yellow tubular blossoms.

CORYDALIS lutea
Corydalis

CRAMBE cordifolia
Colewort

CRAMBE

Colewort
* **Summer**
* **Fast/long display**
* **Ht: 2m/7ft**

Only a cabbage in fancy-dress really, **Crambe cordifolia** is stunning at the back of the border, or naturalized in semi-shade. Everything about it is enormous except the flowers. In the soil it likes (rich, well-drained, neutral to alkaline), it will shoot up more than 2m with deeply lobed heart-shaped basal leaves all of 60cm in diameter. Come early spring, the stout flower-stems begin to rise, branching and re-branching until they reach their maximum height, when they burst into a cloud of tiny, fragrant white 4-petalled flowers, rather like Virginia Stock. **Crambe** is propagated by root division in earliest spring or may be grown from spring-sown seed which will take about three years to reach flowering size. Like others of the cabbage family, they are attractive to slugs, snails and caterpillars.

CYNARA

Cardoon
* **Spring – autumn**
* **Average/long display** C T
* **Ht: 2.5m/8ft**

Tall, spectacular Cardoons are great value in the larger perennial border or may be used as feature plants almost anywhere. Grown mostly from spring-planted suckers, they soon sprout metre-long silvery leaves, looking much like a silver treefern. As the lower leaves flop on the ground, others appear in their place until you have an enormous rosette over 2m in diameter. Finally, after regular water and feeding, the heavy flower stalks begin to rise and keep growing until they're taller than any gardener. At full summer height, the buds develop into mauve blooms like giant scotch thistles. These consist of multiple rows of spiny, overlapping bracts topped with a pompon of long-stamened tubular flowers. Botanically, the Cardoon is known as **Cynara cardunculus,** and it's no accident the blooms resemble that great delicacy, the Globe Artichoke, for those are the buds of related **C. scolymus.** Grow the Cardoon in deep, heavily enriched soil with free drainage — and as a bonus you can cook and eat the edible root and leaf-stalks. Grow them from spring seed too, but they won't reach flowering size the first year. Cardoons die back and look very sad in winter — but they can easily be tidied up.

DELPHINIUM

Candle Larkspur
* **Summer – autumn**
* **Fast/long display** ☼ C T
* **Ht: to 2m/6ft**

Think blue — think **Delphiniums!** These tall and stately perennials of cooler climate gardens are one of the glories of the summer border, producing great clumps of hand-shaped leaves ingeniously divided in a dozen different ways, and mostly of a pale, elegant green. From among them appear heavy spire-like stems completely covered with 3cm cup-shaped blooms in

CYNARA cardunculus
Cardoon

CYNARA cardunculus
Cardoon (foliage)

DELPHINIUM *nudicaule*
Scarlet Larkspur

DELPHINIUM X 'Mighty Atom'

DELPHINIUM (continued)

every imaginable shade of blue and mauve, from palest baby-blue to darkest indigo. Earlier hybrids were single, but now, with hybridists busy year after year, we have semi-double and ruffled varieties — some even fully double — while the range of colours has been widened to include white, pink and (even more recently) a few in lemon and cream shades. All of these are hybrids of Eurasian **D. elatum** crossed with several other species, and although (as noted elsewhere in this series) they can be grown as annuals from seed, the really spectacular cultivars come true only from vegetative propagation. Crowns or clumps, consisting of a mass of fleshy roots, can be purchased in autumn or early spring from specialist nurserymen. These are planted in deep, slightly alkaline soil in full sun, but preferably sheltered by taller plants or hedges, for they are very prone to wind damage without strong staking. They can be propagated too from cuttings 10cm long, taken as close as possible to the rootstock when growth has begun in spring. These are struck in a sand/peat mixture under glass, set out in a nursery area when rooted, and transplanted to final position in late summer for bloom the following year. If you wish to grow from seed, sow under glass in winter at a temperature of 18-24°C/65-75°F, when germination takes about two weeks. Prick the young seedlings into boxes and plant out in spring or autumn. Cut the main flower spike for indoor use, or when faded, and smaller spikes will often appear towards autumn. Many other perennial **Delphinium** species are also grown, including the dwarf Californian **D. nudicaule** with scarlet flowers. This has a long blooming season during spring and summer, and is grown from fresh summer seed and planted out in autumn for bloom the following season. This species can cope with semi-shade and looks great in a naturalized woodland setting.

DELPHINIUM *elatum* hybrids ▶
at Chelsea Flower Show

DIANTHUS arenarius
Prussian Pink

DIANTHUS X *allwoodii*
Hybrid Pink

DIANTHUS deltoides
Maiden Pink

DIANTHUS

Carnation, Pinks, Gillyflower
* **Summer – autumn**
* **Aveage/long display**
* **Ht: 20-100cm/28-36in**

The name **Dianthus** means divine or heavenly flower, and has been used since the days of ancient Greece. Whether we call them Pinks, Carnations or (as in the Middle Ages) Gillyflowers, all of the illustrated flowers are perennial species of the genus. The Perpetual-flowering Carnations (**D.** X **caryophyllus** hybrids) can be grown under glass to produce cutting blooms the entire year. They can be propagated from winter seed, but most named cultivars are grown from 15cm winter cuttings of healthy side shoots with 6-7 pairs of leaves. Leaves are cut in half, the cuttings inserted in pots of sharp sand, and kept at 16-18°C/61-64°F until rooted. These are potted up, then planted out in late spring. Pinching will produce bushier growth. They love full sun, perfect drainage and grow best in a neutral, sandy soil. Carnations are often grown in wire supporting frames to prevent the top-

DIANTHUS caryophyllus
Sim Hybrid Carnations

DIANTHUS X 'Earl of Essex'
Clove Pink

heavy blooms from flopping. Regular water and fortnightly feeding as flower buds develop will produce fine blooms, but watch for aphids, thrip and caterpillars. Smaller **D. plumarius** includes all the old-fashioned clove-scented Pinks. They are lower, untidier plants, but propagated in the same way and used at the front of the border, or in rockeries. Regular dead-heading will produce a profusion of blooms. The **D. X allwoodii** hybrids are relatively modern productions, cross the older Pinks with modern Carnations. They are mostly in a limited range of pinks and reds, often with a contrasting eye. **D. arenarius** and **D. deltoides** are both dwarf, mat-forming plants, easily grown from seed or cuttings. Ideal in rockeries or as ground cover, they do well in a gritty soil, bloom best when you use a high-potassium fertilizer. Regular water is needed, and **D. arenarius** will be happier in semi-shade.

57

DIASCIA

Twin Flower
* **Summer**
* **Average/short display**
* **Ht: 22-45cm/8-18in**

Not very common anywhere except in their native South Africa, the 20-odd species of **Diascia** (both annual and perennial) are useful additions to the temperate garden. Related to **Linaria, Nemesia** and **Torenia,** all of which they resemble in some degree, they do best in a sunny position in almost any soil, and have no special requirements beyond a light ration of fertilizer when flowers are forming, and regular water. Sow seed early spring, plant out later for summer bloom. Pinching out will make the plants bushier, and a second flush can be promoted when the stems of twin-spurred pink flowers are cut back after they fade.

DIASCIA rigescens
Twin Flower

DICENTRA spectabilis
Bleeding Heart

DICENTRA

Bleeding Heart, Locket Flower
* **Spring – summer**
* **Average/long display**
* **Ht: 45-75cm/1½-2½ft**

Graceful, old-time perennials related to the poppies, the handful of **Dicentra** species can only be grown with success in cool or cold-winter areas. They are delicate herbaceous plants for the semi-shaded shrubbery with deep, woodsy soil, and shrivel up in full sun or dry conditions. **D. spectabilis** is the preferred species, native to Japan, but south of the equator you will only find it doing well in gardens of hillside areas. A tangle of fleshy roots when planted in autumn, **Dicentra** sends up ferny green foliage in spring, and then arching stems hung with heart or locket-shaped blossoms. On these, the outer petals are red or pink, the inner white. **Dicentra** can be propagated from winter divisions which must be replanted immediately. Seed should be sown in moist peat and sand, chilled in the refrigerator for 6 weeks, then germinated at a temperature of 16°C/60°F. The plants die back completely in late summer.

58

DICHORISANDRA thyrsiflora
Purple Ginger

DICHORISANDRA

Purple Ginger
* **Summer – autumn**
* **Average/long display**
* **Ht: 60-130cm /2-4ft**

A striking tropical perennial from Brazil, **Dichorisandra thyrsiflora** can be grown in far more temperate climes with winter protection for the succulent stems. It is definitely not frost-hardy. A tall-growing plant — up to 1.3m, it is related to the common Wandering Jews. Grow under the shade of trees, in shade houses or containerized on a sheltered patio. Well-drained soil with plenty of leaf-mould is ideal. Regular water and high humidity are expected in summer, tapering right off in winter. It can be grown from seed, cuttings, root divisions or by detaching the small, rooted plantlets that form on main stems. The glossy green leaves are spirally arranged, with vivid violet blooms borne profusely in tall spikes.

DICLIPTERA

Orange Justicia
* **Spring – autumn**
* **Average/long display**
* **Ht: 25cm/12in**

A charming but little-known dwarf shrubby perennial for the warm-climate rock garden or bank, Uruguayan **Dicliptera suberecta** retains a reminder of earlier nomenclature and relationships in the popular name Orange Justicia. Grow it in well-drained sandy soil in a sun-drenched position, and propagate from spring cuttings struck in sharp sand. When not in bloom, **Dicliptera** forms a neat mound of velvety-grey compact foliage — but then, arching flower stems develop and suddenly the whole plant is covered is a mass of firecracker-orange tubular blossom. It can also be grown in pots or baskets for terrace display — needs plenty of water as the flowers develop.

DICLIPTERA suberecta
Orange Justicia

DICTAMNUS albus
Burning Bush

DICTAMNUS

Gas Plant, Burning Bush, Dittany, Fraxinella
* **Summer**
* **Average/long display**
* **Ht: 80cm-1m/2½ to 3ft/spreading**

This may not be the burning bush that Moses ran across, but it will certainly do until the real thing comes along! A strongly aromatic herbaceous perennial with shining, dark-green compound leaves, it is an ornament to any border and has a peculiarity that will fascinate your friends and charm the children to distraction. In hot, still weather, the entire plant exudes volatile oil in the form of an invisible vapour. One touch of a match near the base of a flower spike and pff! — a sudden burst of flame may startle you, but won't damage the flowers at all. A native of southern Europe and Asia, **Dictamnus albus** bears attractive long-stemmed white blooms in terminal racemes; likes a well-drained soil rich in leafmould, with regular water. It may be propagated from root-cuttings taken in early spring or from seed sown outdoors in late autumn for spring germination. Plant at 1m spacings.

DODECATHEON meadia
Shooting Star

DODECATHEON

Shooting Star
* **Spring – summer**
* **Average /long display**
* **Ht: 30-45cm /12-18in**
Beautiful woodsy primula-relatives from North America, **Dodecatheons** are not often seen in gardens of the southern hemisphere, but would be quite at home in hillside or mountain areas — for they do need cold weather. To raise from seed, it is necessary to sprinkle on a moist soil mix and keep in the freezer for three weeks. Then, placing the tray in a propagator, raise the temperature to 21°C/70°F for up to a month, when germination should take place. When the seedlings are large enough to prick out, grow them on under glass for two years before planting out. Established plants can be divided early in autumn. **Dodecatheon meadia** is most commonly seen romping away in leafy, well-drained soil to form handsome rosettes of light green, toothed, primula-type leaves. From these, the 45cm flower stalks pop up in late spring, each topped with an umbel of cyclamen-pink 2.5cm blooms whose petals are strongly reflexed from a yellow centre. They do in fact look like cyclamen blooms. All 30-odd species of **Dodecatheon** resent disturbance.

DORONICUM

Leopard's Bane
* **Spring – autumn**
* **Fast / long blooming**
* **Ht: 30-100cm / 1-3ft**

Twentyfive species in the enormous daisy family, Leopard's Banes or **Doronicum** grow wild from England to Iran. They like deep, damp soil, should be planted 30-45cm apart in a position with morning sun or in part-shaded drifts under trees. They are most variable, some growing from fibrous roots, others from runners. Leaves may be heart or kidney shaped, acute, obtuse or elongated.

Heights vary from 30-100cm. But all species have glorious golden-yellow daisy flowers with brilliantly shining petals, very suitable for cutting and borne freely on young plants. To propagate from existing plants, it is merely necessary to lift, divide and replant the root masses between autumn and spring every 2-3 years. They can also be raised from seed sown right on the surface of the seed-raising mix and dampened. Do not cover with soil! Germination takes 2-3 weeks at a temperature of 21°C/70°F. Illustrated **Doronicum plantagineum** should be dead-headed regularly, and will reward with a second blooming in autumn. Cut right back in late winter.

DORONICUM plantagineum
Leopard's Bane

ECHINACEA

Purple Coneflower
* **Summer – autumn**
* **Average/long blooming**
* **Ht: 130-150cm/4-5ft**

C T

Native to the great prairies of North America, the showy Purple Coneflower prefers plenty of sun and will thrive in average garden soil with good drainage. It will even tolerate dry conditions and exposure to wind and should do well both inland and in coastal gardens. Most commonly grown of only three species, **Echinacea purpurea** can be multiplied from autumn divisions, or from winter root-cuttings which can be grown on under glass for planting out when the weather is warm. Seed is sown in winter at a temperature of 20-24°C/68-75°F and will flower late the following season. Regular dead-heading will prolong the display, and in colder climates the entire plant can be cut back in late autumn. It is root-hardy to frost.

ECHINACEA purpurea
Purple Coneflower

ECHINOPS ritro
Small Globe Thistle

ECHINOPS

Globe Thistle
* **Summer**
* **Fast/long display**
* **Ht: 45-120cm/18-48in**

C T

Found naturally from the Mediterranean eastwards as far as India, many of the 100-odd species of **Echinops** or Globe Thistles have been tamed to become favourite plants worldwide. Most popular species are the 120cm **E. banaticus** from Hungary, and the smaller 90cm **E. ritro** which is found in southern Europe and in Asia. Both can be grown from root divisions taken in colder weather, or from seed germinated at a temperature of 24°C/75°F. Young plants should appear in 2-3 weeks and are later planted out at 60cm spacings. **Echinops** like plenty of water over the blooming period, which will continue if flowers are cut regularly. Those of **E. ritro** have a steely lustre and may be cut and dried for winter decoration. Leaves are thistle-like and downy beneath, and the plants are very drought-resistant.

ECHIUM

Pride of Madeira
* **Spring – summer**
* **Fast/long display**
* **Ht: 1-2m/3-6ft/spreading**

☼ T

Tall, striking, blue, mauve and pink-spired perennials from the Mediterranean and several Atlantic islands, **Echiums** are all easy to grow, though flowering best in poor-quality soil. When the going is too rich or damp they bolt to foliage and grow unwieldy. The Pride of Madeira, **E. fastuosum**, makes a splendid feature plant in seaside gardens, for its long-pointed, parallel-veined leaves are covered with salt-resistant, silver-silky hairs. Leaves are borne in great profusion all up the rather woody branches, each of which is tipped in late spring and summer with a long panicle of purple-blue, bell-shaped flowers, very honey-rich and attractive to bees. They are propagated altogether too easily from seed sown in the final position almost any time, and faded flower heads should be pruned and burned before they have a chance to self-seed in every direction. The plants should be pruned lightly to prevent undue legginess. Not at all frost-hardy.

ECHIUM fastuosum
Pride of Madeira

EPILOBIUM

Fireweed, French Willow, Willow Herb
* **Summer**
* **Fast/long display**
* **Ht: 1-2m/3-6ft**

Some of the most invasive perennials, **Epilobiums** are native to the northern hemisphere with a few outliers in New Zealand. Most widely seen is lovely **Epilobium angustifolium** whose popularity can best be judged by its wide range of popular names, of which Fireweed, French Willow, Rose Bay, Wickup and Willow Herb are only a few. Plant from divisions; from grown-on cuttings of spring basal shoots; or from spring-sown seed, which should be pricked out after germination and set in final position also in autumn. Any light, well-drained soil suits, and regular water is a necessity. The tall stems, clothed in willowy foliage, are topped in summer with terminal racemes of open, rose-pink flowers like Evening Primroses, to which they are related.

EPILOBIUM angustifolium
Fireweed

EPIMEDIUM

Bishops' Hats, Barrenwort
* **Spring**
* **Average/long display**
* **Ht: 20cm/8in/spreading**

Hardy dwarf perennials for large rockeries or wild gardens, the 20-odd species of **Epimedium** are evergreen, make a charming display for most of the year, different in every season. They grow from spreading underground roots which send up the foliage on wiry stems in early spring. Leaves of the hybrid **E. X youngianum** each consist of a number of heart-shaped leaflets, prickly edged and brightly marked with red. In late spring, when bright green, they are joined by wiry, compact stems of tiny white or pink flowers — something like 1cm daffodils. In autumn, the leaves turn orange and red. Plant from spring or autumn divisions, or sow seed in summer soon after ripening. Old or damaged leaves should be removed in spring to accent the flower display.

EPIMEDIUM X youngianum
Bishops' Hats

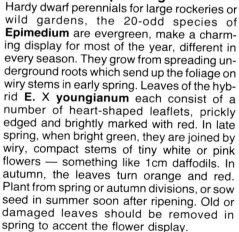

ERIGERON

Fleabane, Midsummer Aster,
Vittadenia
* **Mostly summer**
* **Fast/long display**
* **Ht: 15-60cm/6-24in/spreading**

A large and variable genus of the daisy family, showy **Erigerons** differ from other daisy genera in surrounding their compound flower heads with two or more rows of fine, thread-like petals (or ray florets as they are often called). The most popular species for perennial border work are all North American, relatively low-growing plants that quickly form large clumps from division in autumn or early spring. Prairie plants, they prefer a sandy, light-textured soil of average to poor quality. They also need regular water and good drainage. **Erigerons** can be raised from seed, which is sown either outdoors in early spring or under controlled conditions, when germination will take place in 2-3 weeks at a constant 13°C/55°F. Young seedlings should be pricked out and grown on until they can safely be planted at 30cm intervals. The

ERIGERON X 'Darkest of All'
Fleabane

ERIGERON speciosus 'Dimity'
Quaker Daisy

ERIGERON speciosus
Fleabane

ERIGERON karvinskianus
Vittadenia

most popular bedding species is **E. speciosus** from the western United States, where it is often called the Midsummer Aster. It has many colour varieties including pale and deep pink, pale blue, mauve and purple. Also North American is **E. auranticus,** the Double Orange Daisy. This is best used as a rock garden plant as it rarely passes 22cm in height. All these North American species make good cut flowers and bloom prolifically when regularly dead-headed. In cold areas they should be cut back to the ground in late autumn; where the climate is more temperate they will remain evergreen. Mexican **E. karvinskianus** is different altogether, blooming year round in warmer climates. It is a wiry, sub-shrubby sort of plant, spreading widely with trailing 1m stems of 2cm white daisy flowers. These fade to pink and finally wine red. Useful for ground cover or rockery work, it should be cut back hard from time to time to prevent excessive self-seeding. Drought-resistant, it enjoys rooting among stones.

67

ERYNGIUM

Eryngo, Sea Holly
* **Summer**
* **Average/long display** ☼ [C] [T]
* **Ht: 30-60cm/1-2ft**

Spiky, formidable looking members of the carrot family, the **Eryngiums** or Sea Hollies are found on every continent, but most cultivated species come from Europe or North America. Valued for their interesting foliage and spiny-collared blooms which have a bluish metallic sheen, all can be grown from winter root-cuttings planted under glass until they produce foliage. These are planted out the following autumn. Seed germinates in 5-10 days when sown at a temperature of 24°C/75°F. They prefer a dry, sandy soil with perfect drainage, and should be watered regularly but lightly. Handle with care! Flower stems may be dried for winter decoration indoors.

ERYNGIUM dichotomum
Eryngo

ERYNGIUM bourgatii
Sea Holly

ERYSIMUM perovskianum
Treacle Mustard

ERYSIMUM X linifolium
Blister Cress

ERYSIMUM

Blister Cress, Treacle Mustard
* **Spring – summer**
* **Fast/long display**   ☼ C T
* **Ht: 18-60cm/6-24in**

The popular names of these interesting perennials remind us that they once had medicinal uses as counter-irritants. Members of the cress family, they are obviously close relatives of the fragrant wallflower, and there are about 80 species found in all parts of the northern hemisphere, where they thrive in areas with poor soil. In the garden, give them a well-drained, average loam with regular water, and they'll turn on a dazzling display for months on end. **Erysimum** species may be propagated from heeled cuttings taken in summer. These are rooted under glass in a sand-peat mixture, potted up into a richer soil and set out the following spring. They can also be raised from seed, and young seedlings are planted out in autumn in milder areas — or early spring where the winters are cold. When established, they will self-seed freely.

69

EUPHORBIA griffithii 'Fireglow'
Red Spurge

EUPHORBIA wulfenii
Poison Spurge

EUPHORBIA

Spurge
* **Spring – summer**
* **Average /long display**
* **Ht: 45-120cm /18-48in**

Some 1500 species are included in the genus **Euphorbia** — annuals, perennials, shrubs, succulents and cactus-like plants, even a few trees. Most have little or no resemblance to one another, and come from all corners of the world. What do they all have in common then, apart from the name? First, an unpleasant milky sap, usually poisonous. Second, spectacular flower-like arrangements which are not flowers at all, but a series of highly coloured bracts or modified leaves surrounding a group of tiny, simple flowers, some male, some female. The shrubby tropical species **E. pulcherrima** (the Poinsettia, from Mexico) and **E. milii** (the Crown of Thorns, from Malagasy) are undoubtedly the showiest of the genus and grown in warm climate gardens worldwide. But here we are concerned with the many perennial species which are valued for bed and border work in cooler climates. The first of these is **E. griffithii,** a true herbaceous perennial from the Himalayas that makes a spectacular show when mass planted at 60cm spacing. It is grown from basal cuttings or seed, the former taken in spring, rooted and re-planted in autumn. The latter are sown and planted in the same season. Growing to 70cm, it has willowy, pink-veined leaves and heads of vivid orange-scarlet bracts. The European **E. wulfenii** is a shrubbier plant growing to 130cm, each stem clothed with linear, blue-green foliage. Its inflores-cence is in the form of a columnar panicle with the florets surrounded by yellow and green bracts. The Cushion Euphorbia, **E. polychroma,** is a bushy evergreen sub-shrub that makes neat mounds of bright green ovate foliage. It is decked with small multiple heads of bright yellow bracts in late spring. All perennial **Euphorbias** can be propagated from division between autumn and spring, or from seed or cuttings as de-tailed above. Erect flower stems of all pe-rennial species are cut back to the ground in autumn to keep the plants compact and stimulate new growth.

EUPHORBIA polychroma
Cushion Euphorbia

FILIPENDULA

Meadowsweet
* **Summer**
* **Slow/long display**
* **Ht: 130-250cm/4-8ft**

Related to both **Aruncus** and the shrubby **Spiraeas**, 10 species of **Filipendula** are included in the rose family. Their striking leaves are very large, 3-5 lobed, doubly serrated and diagonally pleated. **Filipendulas** thrive at the back of the larger perennial border provided the soil does not dry out, but look and grow even better in waterside positions where the soil is both damp and well-drained. Propagate by dividing the crowns around winter. They can be raised from seed sown in early spring, but may take 3 years to reach flowering size. Then, they produce plumes of tiny fragrant flowers each year in early summer. Watch for powdery mildew among the dense foliage, and cut back to the ground in winter in colder areas.

FILIPENDULA camschatica
Meadowsweet

GALEGA officinalis
Goat's Rue

GALEGA

Goat's Rue
* **Summer**
* **Fast/long display**
* **Ht: 1-1.5m/3-5ft**

These easy-to-grow perennials resemble the farmer's lucerne, and from their quaint oldtime popular name, one must wonder if they have the same bloating effect on ruminant beasts! **Galega officinalis** grows wild right across the goat country of southern Europe and Asia Minor, but is at home in any deep soil where it will thrive for years without division. It does even better of course with special feeding and plenty of water, growing into great mounds of handsome pinnate foliage; each leaf having up to 17 leaflets. The flowers appear in showy spikes from the leaf axils during summer. They are typically pea-shaped; mauve, pink or white according to variety. Propagate by dividing the roots from autumn to spring, and cut faded flower stems to the ground.

GENTIANA macrophylla
Large-leaf Gentian

GENTIANA lutea
Yellow Gentian

GENTIANA

Gentian
* **Summer**
* **Slow/long season**
* **Ht: 15-150cm/6-60in**

☼ C T

Since Gentian is a shade of blue, we might imagine all **Gentianas** bloomed in that colour. But there are red, white and yellow flowering species as well, over 350 of them scattered around the cool-temperate alpine areas of the world. All enjoy a damp, gravelly soil that drains well, and are often planted in sloping hillside gardens. Nearly all species are propagated by division in early spring. They can also be grown from autumn-sown seed which is first frozen for three weeks, then germinated at a constant 24°C/75°F. This may take a month. Seedlings are pricked out, potted up singly for planting out the following autumn. They were named for Gentius, a king of Illyria who discovered the value of their bitter roots which are still used medicinally.

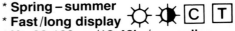

GERANIUM

Cranesbill
* **Spring – summer**
* **Fast/long display** ☼ ☀ C T
* **Ht: 30-120cm /12-48in /spreading**

It is entirely possible that the majority of the world's **Geranium** hobbyists have never seen one in their lives! For the entire range of plants popularly known as Scented, Fancy Leaf, Ivy and Martha Washington Geraniums do not belong to the genus at all, and you will find them listed correctly, later in this book as **Pelargoniums.** But yes, there are real **Geraniums,** botanically so-named, but popularly called Cranesbills on account of the long, beak-like projection on their seeds. True **Geraniums** include some 300 species of perennial plants found all over the world in cool, temperate and alpine regions. They are used mostly in the rock garden, as informal ground covers or as loose mounding plants for the front of

GERANIUM psilostemon
Armenian Cranesbill

GERANIUM sylvaticum
Forest Cranesbill

GERANIUM pratense
Meadow Cranesbill

GERANIUM palmatum
Canary Island Geranium

the border. Exceptions among those pictured are **G. palmatum,** the Canary Island Geranium, which may grow to 70cm and is used for bedding. It self-sows readily in semi-shade. **G. pratense,** too, grows quite tall and is used for mass planting. It has delicate, deeply-lobed foliage and blue flowers in profusion. All species like a damp, well-drained soil and are lifted for division in winter before being immediately replanted. Seed should be sown fresh at a temperature of 21°C/70°F and will take up to 40 days to germinate. The young plants are potted up and ultimately planted out in autumn at 25cm intervals. **G. psilostemon** grows to 60cm, has heart-shaped 5-lobed leaves and black-centred magenta blooms. **G. sylvaticum,** decked with loose clusters of lavender, white or pink blooms in late spring, grows from a creeping rootstock. Its leaves are deeply 7-lobed, each lobe being further toothed. Snipping back faded flower stems keeps **Geraniums** tidy and encourages further bloom.

GERBERA

Transvaal or Barberton Daisy
* **Spring – autumn**
* **Fast/long blooming**
* **Ht: 45-50cm/18-20in**

Unequalled as cut flowers, the splendid **Gerberas** are surely the most decorative of all daisies, with a wide colour range from crimson to pink, yellow and many other tones both bright and subdued. Both single and double hybrids have been bred from the original Barberton Daisy, a small orange species from the Transvaal, though other species are found here and there around the Indian Ocean. **Gerberas** are not frost-hardy, demand full sun and need perfect drainage. Plant from divisions in autumn, or grow from seed germinated at 21°C/70°F in early spring without soil covering. They are in no hurry to sprout and a month may pass before there is any sign of life. **Gerberas** form large clumps — plant them a good 60cm apart.

GERBERA jamesonii
Barberton Daisy

GERBERA hybrid
Transvaal Daisy

GEUM rivale
Water Avens

GEUM

Avens, Indian Chocolate
* **Spring – summer**
* **Average /long display**
* **Ht: 15-60cm /6-24in /spreading**

Less often seen these days of mini-gardens, old-fashioned **Geums** produce masses of red, orange and yellow flowers, but do require sprawling room.

The once-popular bedding species in mixed colours is **Geum quellyou** (formerly **G. chiloense**) from South America. But in smaller gardens the illustrated **G. coccineum** from Asia Minor is a better gamble. It grows to 35cm and flowers are often larger. **G. X borisii** is an even smaller plant, rarely passing 30cm and with orange blooms. The Water Avens, **G. rivale,** is found all over the northern hemisphere and prefers damp soil. Blooms are pale apricot, buds purple. All **Geums** can be propagated from division in early spring. Seed can be sown in winter, and will germinate in a month at temperatures of around 20-30°C /68-86°F.

GEUM coccineum
Dwarf Avens

GUNNERA manicata

GYPSOPHILA repens 'Rosea'
Baby's Breath

GUNNERA

Gunnera
* **Spring**
* **Fast/short display**
* **Ht: 2.5-300cm/1-120in**
As with many other plant genera, the species of **Gunnera** are almost equally divided between South America and New Zealand — suggesting an earlier continental connection. The big difference is in size. While New Zealand **Gunneras** are small mat-forming plants, those from South America are gigantic! What they have in common is a love of water, and all do best alongside pools and streams. Illustrated **G. manicata** from Brazil may reach 3m in height, sprouting enormous prickly-stemmed rough-textured leaves. These spring from a rootstock larger than a human body, and almost hide the spring flower display which consists of a cone-shaped panicle of insignificant greenish blooms. **Gunnera** is propagated by division of the small crowns that form around the base of old plants. Mulch roots in colder climates.

GYPSOPHILA

Baby's Breath, Chalk Plant
* **Summer**
* **Fast/long display**
* **Ht: to 25cm/10in/spreading**
A dainty perennial cousin of the popular annual **Gypsophila, G. repens** is a small sub-shrubby perennial that forms large mats of many-branched wiry stems with narrow grey-green leaves. The tiny 6mm flowers vary from white to pink and appear in loose bunches all over the plant right through summer. It is propagated from 5cm spring cuttings of small lateral shoots. These are rooted in a sand/peat mixture before planting out in early autumn. Like all **Gypsophilas,** Baby's Breath prefers well-drained alkaline soil and needs little water. It is a popular rockery subject and will bloom repeatedly if flower stems are sheared back after they fade.

HELIANTHEMUM

Sun Rose
* **Spring – summer**
* **Average/long display** ☼ C T
* **Ht: 10-45cm/4-18in/spreading**

Small relatives of the handsome, shrubby **Cistus** or rock roses, **Helianthemums** are classed as sub-shrubby perennials. They are low, mound-forming evergreen plants with attractive foliage varying from deep to greyish green, and when well sited in fast-draining, slightly alkaline soil burst into a blaze of summer colour that will last for months. Plant in full sun during winter and shear back hard after blooms have faded to promote a second flush and prevent their spreading all over nearby plants. Heeled 7.5cm cuttings of lateral shoots taken in summer will root rapidly in a sand/peat mix and should be pinched out to develop a bushy habit. Plant out the following spring. Watch for powdery mildew in hot weather.

HELIANTHEMUM nummularium 'Golden' Yellow Sun Rose

HELIANTHEMUM 'Wisley Pink'

HELIANTHUS X *multiflorus*
Double Sunflower

HELIANTHUS

Sunflower
* **Summer – autumn**
* **Fast/long blooming**
* **Ht: 1.5m/5ft/bushy**

☼ C T

A hybrid between the giant Annual Sunflower **(Helianthus annuus)** and the perennial Thin-leaf Sunflower **(H. de-capetalus),** the handsome **H.** X **multi-florus** is a stunning addition to the large bed or border. It has rough-textured ovate leaves up to 25cm in length and 12cm orange-yellow daisy flowers with a varying degree of doubleness. Sometimes the many petals are centred with the usual mass of sunflower florets in the form of a disc, sometimes not, so it is wisest to prop-

agate from divisions, which are lifted and replanted in the cooler months. Like the other large sunflowers it needs a deep, rich, well-drained soil in a position that guarantees a maximum of sunlight — unlike the taller species it rarely needs staking except in exposed positions. Dead-head regularly or cut for indoor display to ensure continued bloom, and be sure to divide at least every three years, for the double sunflowers tend to revert to a single type if left undisturbed for too long, The plants are rather prone to grey mould fungus in wetter climates, and if this occurs, should be thoroughly drenched with a fungicide at the recommended strength. Caterpillars may damage the blooms, but otherwise they are trouble free. Soak well in the growing season.

HELICHRYSUM

Straw Flower, Everlasting
* **Spring – summer**˙
* **Average/long display**
* **Ht: 5-60cm/1-24in/spreading**

C T H

Popular annual **Helichrysums** have been dealt with in a companion volume, but there are perennial types, mostly native to Australasia and South Africa. Like the annuals, these flourish in any well-drained soil in full sunlight, and are especially valuable in hot dry areas. Australia's **H. apiculatum** is a woody-based perennial with silvery-green foliage and small golden blooms borne in terminal clusters up to 5cm in diameter. It is propagated from rooted summer cuttings, taken with a heel. South African **H. milfordiae** is a dwarf perennial forming dense cushions of silvery foliage that are starred with yellow-centred white blooms 3cm in diameter. In wet climates it is grown under glass.

HELICHRYSUM apiculatum
Everlasting

HELICHRYSUM milfordiae
Silver Straw Flower

HELIOPSIS

Ox-Eye
* **Summer – autumn**
* **Fast /long display**
* **Ht: 1-2m /3-6ft /spreading**

Another fine North American daisy genus that puts on a dazzling display in the summer border or naturalized in wild parts of the garden, **Heliopsis** will grow in any soil and are particularly useful in dry areas where their blooming will continue for months with a minimum of precious water. They are commonly planted from root divisions taken in cold weather, but may be grown from seed which will germinate under glass at a temperature of 21°C/70°F. If started early enough, the plants will bloom the first year. They should be set out 60cm apart, preferably in a moist, but well-drained position. Regular dead-heading will prolong the display and flower stems should be cut back to ground level in late autumn. **H. scabra incomparabilis** has semi-double blooms of orange-yellow.

HELIOPSIS scabra incomparabilis
Heliopsis

HELIOPSIS helianthoides
Ox-Eye

HELIOTROPIUM arborescens
Cherry Pie

HELIOTROPIUM X aureum
Golden Heliotrope

HELIOTROPIUM

Heliotrope, Cherry Pie
* **Spring – autumn**
* **Fast / long display** ☼ ☀ C T
* **Ht: to 120cm / 4 ft / spreading**

Sweetly fragrant, the old-time Heliotrope or Cherry Pie of cottage gardens is actually an exotic South African import — tender to frost and fast-growing in mild climates. So fast that many people set out cuttings in early spring and treat them as annuals. It is one of those borderline plants, listed by some authorities as sub-shrub, by others as a shrubby perennial. Heliotrope grows in any enriched, well-drained garden soil in full sun, but enjoys humidity. So in *very* hot dry areas they are best raised in semi-shade and the foliage sprinkled regularly. Give them weak liquid fertilizer continually during the growing season, and cut back by at least half in very early spring.

HELLEBORUS orientalis
Lenten Rose, Hellebore

HELLEBORUS corsicus
Corsican Hellebore

HELLEBORUS

Winter Rose, Hellebore
* **Winter – spring**
* **Slow /long display**
* **Ht: 25-60cm /10-24in**

Useful winter and spring flowering perennials for the cooler climate, Hellebores provide unusual and exciting colorations for the flower arranger. Apple green, greenish-white and many shades of purple are the principal tones. Plant them in drifts or massed in the semi-shade of deciduous trees during autumn, making sure the soil is heavily enriched with organic matter. Give them several years to become established and they'll reward you year after year with masses of fascinating flowers during the colder months when blooms can be hard to come by. All species of **Helleborus** are native to southern Europe and western Asia, but they have found popularity all over the globe — even under their European popular names of Lenten Rose and Christmas Rose, which of course are seasonally illogi-

84

cal south of the equator. Roses they are not, but closely related to the **Ranunculus,** and like Miss Greta Garbo, they want to be left alone, although a topdressing of well-rotted compost or manure after flowering seems to have an improving effect. If you wish to multiply them, lift and divide the roots immediately after flowering, risking a year's loss of bloom. Ripened seed can be sown in early summer, under glass. Pricked out when large enough, and grown on, the seedlings will be unlikely to flower before the third year. Hellebores are evergreen, and hold their handsome, deeply-lobed and divided leaves all year, those of **Helleborus corsicus** being rather spiny. One cardinal rule, never let the plants dry out over the summer months, keep moist always.

HELLEBORUS foetidus
Stinking Hellebore

HELLEBORUS niger
Winter Rose, Christmas Rose

HETEROCENTRON roseum
Heeria rosea

HETEROCENTRON

(syn HEERIA)

* **Autumn – winter**
* **Slow /short display**
* **Ht: to 1m /3ft**

Best known in warm-climate gardens for the brilliantly-flowered groundcover known as Spanish Shawl, the genus **Heterocentron** includes several shrubby perennial species of great value in warm and temperate gardens. Illustrated **H. roseum** (known for many years as **Heeria rosea**) is a handsome plant that may reach 1m in favourable conditions. Native to Mexico and Guatemala, it does best in a sandy soil enriched with peat, and demands regular water. It is best propagated from root divisions or cuttings in early spring and spreads by means of suckers. In autumn, the stems of red-edged elliptical leaves are topped with panicles of bright cerise 2.5cm flowers, rather like those of the creeping species. Old flower stems may be cut back in early spring.

HEUCHERA americana
Alum Root

HEUCHERA

Coral Bells, Alum Root
* **Spring – summer**
* **Fast /long display**
* **Ht: 45cm /18in /spreading**

Heuchera species seem somewhat out of fashion these days and are often hard to find. If you are lucky enough, they make splendid edgings for perennial borders or a charming massed planting. Some species are grown specifically for their rosettes of heart-shaped, interestingly marked foliage, the flowers being snipped away. But the two illustrated species produce a bonus of 45cm flower stems that are much valued by arrangers. Plant in autumn in light, neutral to alkaline soil in full sun, except in dry climates where light tree-shade is recommended. They should be divided every third year. Seed is somewhat unreliable, but can be sown indoors at a temperature of 13°C/55°F. Germination should take about two weeks. Bloom can be prolonged by removing spent flower stems.

HEUCHERA sanguinea
Coral Bells

HIBISCUS

Swamp Rose Mallow, Perennial
Hibiscus
* **Summer**
* **Fast/long display**
* **Ht: 1-2.4m/3-8ft**

☼ C T

Where climates are not warm enough for
the splendid Hawaiian hybrid **Hibiscus** to
do their thing, gardeners must be content
with **Hibiscus moscheutos,** an herbaceous perennial species from the eastern United States. These flower in a respectable
colour range of white, pink and red, usually
with contrasting centres, and are planted
from division in autumn or spring. Deep,
damp soil is best, enriched with compost
and leafmould, and they should be fed
complete fertilizer every 6 weeks during the
growing season. Staking will probably be
required unless the clumps are dense.
Never allow to dry out, and cut back hard in
winter.

HIBISCUS moscheutos
Swamp Rose Mallow

HOUTTUYNIA

Polypora
* **Summer**
* **Fast/long display**
* **Ht: 30-45cm/12-18in/spreading**

There's just one species in this genus of waterloving perennials; it thrives in any damp, semi-shaded position and will even grow in boggy soil or very shallow water. It makes a dense, attractive groundcover but must be watched lest it become too invasive. **Houttuynia** grows from underground runners which spread fast and send up bright red branched stems at intervals. These bear attractive heart-shaped leaves, often stunningly marked in red, and the summer blooms consist of a 1cm cone of tiny flowers surrounded by four white bracts. These are borne at the ends of stem branches. Propagate from spring or autumn divisions, or from seed which is often hard to obtain. It is native to the Himalayan areas of China and mountainous areas of Indonesia and Japan.

HOUTTUYNIA cordata
Polypora

HYLOMECON japonicum
Wood Poppy

HYLOMECON

Wood Poppy
* **Spring – summer**
* **Average/short display**
* **Ht: 30cm/12in/spreading**

A delightful dwarf perennial from woodland areas of Japan and Southeast Asia, **Hylomecon** is again a monotypic species that romps away in deep, acid woodsy soil with plenty of peat and leafmould. Though classed as a member of the poppy family, you'd be hard put to place the relationship until the 5cm 4-petalled golden flowers open in late spring. Its leaves are compound, with 2 or 3 pairs of toothed leaflets and quite hairy when young. Mostly they resemble the foliage of an **Astilbe** or **Helleborus** (which see). Propagate them from autumn divisions or seed sown outdoors in spring in a sheltered position. Keep lightly moist throughout the growing season and cut back in autumn. They are root-hardy in frosty areas.

HYPOESTES

Polka Dot Plant, Freckleface, Velvet Plant

* **Winter – spring**
* **Fast /long display** ☼ ☀ T H
* **Ht: 30-100cm /1-3ft**

If you live in the right climate, you pays your money and you takes your choice! **Hypoestes aristata** gives plenty of bloom and uninteresting foliage, **H. phyllostachya** quite the opposite. The first comes from South Africa, the second from Malagasy, and both of them need a minimum winter temperature of 10°C/50°F to survive. They are not frost-hardy, but in the right climate seem to grow happily in any soil, developing dense, deep-rooted clumps and self-seeding regularly. Shear back the flower stems in autumn and divide the clumps for replanting. Cuttings are also raised easily at this time, though you'll have no need of them once the plants are established. Regular moisture and monthly feeding will produce better foliage on the Freckleface, which should be kept compact.

HYPOESTES aristata
Velvet Plant

HYPOESTES phyllostachya 'Splash'
Freckleface

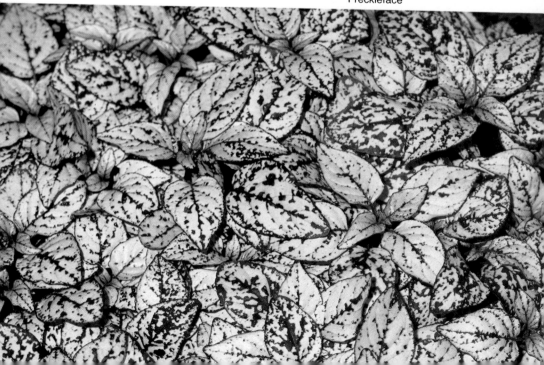

IBERIS

Candytuft
* **Spring – summer**
* **Average/long display**
* **Ht: 10-45cm/4-18in**

Similar but less spectacular than the annual Candytufts, **Iberis sempervirens** is a dwarf, mat-forming plant much used for rock gardens and for edging of perennial borders. A small, spreading plant with several cultivars varying only in height, it will grow in full sun in any ordinary garden soil provided the drainage is good. Normally planted out in the colder months, it can also be grown from seed which is sown under glass at a temperature of 13-18°C/55-65°F, when it will germinate in less than 3 weeks. **Iberis** has trailing stems tipped with rosettes of dark, oblong leaves from which spring flat 5cm heads of white bloom in late spring. Shearing back after bloom will usually stimulate a second flush. They don't appeal to many pests.

IBERIS sempervirens
Perennial Candytuft

INCARVILLEA grandiflora
Pride of China

INCARVILLEA

Pride of China, Hardy Gloxinia
* **Spring – summer**
* **Slow/short display**
* **Ht: 22-45cm/9-18in**

Beautifully marked trumpet-blooms in bright cerise, scarlet or yellow are the main attraction of this perennial genus from high places of Tibet and China. Growing from a mass of fleshy roots, they send up exquisitely formed foliage and elegant flower stems in spring. Some species have fern-like leaves, though in illustrated **Incarvillea grandiflora** they are merely compound with up to 4 pairs of lateral leaflets. Grow them in sun with rich, well-drained soil. Seeds germinate in a month at a temperature of 13-18°C/55-65°F, but will take 3 years to bloom. Best plant out from autumn divisions and mulch the root area in winter.

INULA oculis-christi ▶
Eye of Christ

INULA hirta
Inula

INULA magnifica
Giant Inula

INULA

Eye of Christ
* **Summer**
* **Fast/long display**
* **Ht: 5-180cm/2-72in**

Known and grown since the most ancient of days (their name **Inula** was bestowed by old Roman botanists) this showy genus of daisy flowers included some 60 perennial species from Asia, Africa and Europe, ranging in height from 5cm rock plants to an impressive 180cm. So you can grow them in any part of the garden so long as you like yellow flowers, for they don't come in any other hue! Most will grow in any garden soil so long as it is fertile and moisture-retaining, but they must have full sun. Most of them develop into dense clumps of unbranched stems with broad, basal foliage and spear-shaped stem leaves gradually reducing in size as the stems gain height. The leaves are deeply veined and both they and the stems are hairy (or at least downy) in many species. The style of inflorescence varies from type to type, the daisy-blooms being borne singly, or in corymbs, racemes or panicles. They are propagated by division in spring and autumn, and may also be raised from seed sown as soon as possible after ripening. Under cover, it should germinate in 3 weeks at a temperature range of 13-18°C/55-65°F. Of the illustrated species: **Inula oculis-christi** is relatively small, rarely passing 60cm, with flowers 8.5cm wide; **I. hirta** is even smaller with blooms 7cm in diameter; **I. magnifica,** an Asian species, is altogether larger, reaching 2m in height, with 30cm leaves and multiple heads of orange-centred, cup-shaped flowers borne in corymbs. A peculiarity of all **Inula** species is the multiple row or involucre of heavy bracts at the back of each flower. These are particularly noticeable in the unopened buds. **Inulas** are cut back at season's end and have proven frost-hardy in all parts of England. Whether they would stand up to American winters is problematical, though heavy mulches might help.

JASIONE

Sheep Bit, Shepherd's Scabious, Blue Clover
* **Summer**
* **Average/short display** ☼ ◐ T
* **Ht: 30cm/12in**

Dainty little meadow plants from the Mediterranean area, several species of **Jasione** are grown in rock gardens for their charming clover-like flower heads, which bloom in a particularly attractive shade of jacaranda blue. Perennial **Jasione perennis** is the most popular, growing from a small rosette of hairy leaves that are widest at their outer ends. A sandy, even gravelly soil suits all species best, with perfect drainage. Perennial species are planted out at 30cm intervals and may be divided in autumn. They also grow well from autumn-sown seed, germinating in about 2 weeks at a temperature of 21°C/70°F. Don't over-feed — the plants tend to flop in rich soil.

KNAUTIA

Gypsy Rose, Field Scabious
* **Summer**
* **Fast/long display** ☼ C T
* **Ht: 1m/3ft**

A popular wildflower all around the Mediterranean area and as far east as the Caucasus, **Knautia arvensis** in its wild form is often known as Blue Buttons because of its pale blue, Scabious-lookalike flowers. It was in fact once included in that genus until botanists found some significant differences, and is now grown in a number of colour varieties, yellow, purple and the illustrated 'Alba'. Plant them 25-35cm apart in a sunny position in rich, well-drained soil, preferably slightly alkaline in makeup. They can be propagated from autumn divisions or from seed, sown at 21-24°C/70-75°F, when it will germinate in about 2 weeks. Regular summer water improves flower yield. Staking of taller plants keeps them tidy.

JASIONE perennis
Shepherd's Scabious

KNAUTIA arvensis 'Alba'
Gypsy Rose

93

LACTUCA bourgaei
Sow Thistle

LAMIASTRUM galeobdolon
Yellow Archangel

LACTUCA

(syn MULGEDIUM)

Sow Thistle
* **Summer**
* **Fast/long display**
* **Ht: 2m/6ft**

As I often complain that the vegetable crisper in my refrigerator wasn't designed to hold an average lettuce, it's as well I don't have to cope with this monster. For that's what it is — nothing more or less than a giant, perennial lettuce! Like its smaller, edible cousins, **Lactuca bourgaei** romps away in a light, fertile soil that is moist, neutral and well drained. It is raised the same way from seed, either sown outdoors on the surface in early spring, or, for a head start, indoors, when germination will take 10 days at 19°C/65°F. Prick out when a reasonable size and transplant carefully to the garden later at spacings of 60cm. These tall-growing border plants need lashings of water to produce their panicles of lilac daisy flowers in summer.

LAMIASTRUM

Yellow Archangel
* **Summer**
* **Fast/long display**
* **Ht: to 60cm/2ft/spreading**

Lamiastrum is most commonly grown as a rather loose groundcover in the shade of deciduous trees — and so it did in my own garden until I decided it was determined to take over the whole place. So out it came. But if you have more room than I, it will grow in any moist, shaded area, sending down deep roots that are the devil to get out. It spreads from runners, and in its most attractive form, **L. galeobdolon variegatum** produces long trailing stems of silver-marked, coarsely-toothed, pointed ovate leaves. In early summer, it sends up 60cm flower spikes which produce one or two leaves and a whorl of golden-yellow flowers at every node. These are most attractive. **Lamiastrums** are all too easily propagated from clump divisions and should be sheared back after bloom.

LAMIUM

Dead Nettle, Archangel
* **Spring – summer**
* **Fast/long display**
* **Ht: 15-60cm/6-24in**

Common hedgerow plants and weeds in many parts of Europe and the Middle East, few of the 40 species of **Lamium** have found their way into cultivation, but these few have become worldwide favourites for flowering groundcover in shaded areas, in spite of invasive habits. They are related to and strongly resemble the dreaded stinging nettle, with one important variation — no stinging hairs! And so they have become known to country folk as Dead Nettles. The cultivated species are: **L. album,** the Archangel or Snowflake, which is a densely foliaged 60cm perennial with coarsely-toothed nettlelike leaves and spikes of white flowers arranged in whorls; **L. maculatum,** the Spotted Dead Nettle, which grows only to 45cm, has deeply toothed heart-shaped leaves often spotted white along the midrib, and sports spikes of pink or purple flowers. It has gold and white variegated garden cultivars. **L. orvala,** the Giant Dead Nettle, is less invasive, has purple blooms. All do well in any soil with regular water, and are propagated from winter divisions of the root mass. But give them plenty of room.

LAMIUM maculatum
Spotted Dead Nettle

LATHYRUS grandiflorus
Two-flowered Pea

LATHYRUS

Perennial Pea
* **Spring – summer**
* **Fast/long blooming**
* **Ht: 1-1.8m/3-6ft**

So popular have modern annual Sweet-peas become, many of us have lost sight of the fact that they are only one of some 125 species in the genus, most of the others being perennial. We are familiar perhaps with **Lathyrus latifolius,** the so-called Argentine Pea, which has rather unpleasantly-coloured mauve-pink flowers that are relatively scentless. The most one can say of it is that it climbs and is ever-green in temperate climates. Here is another semi-climbing perennial species, **L. grandiflorus,** with blooms of magnificent rosy-red, and borne in pairs. Grow it from seed sown in spring and planted out the following autumn by an old stump or an evergreen bush, or propagate it from divisions of the rootstock. It will lean or scramble over the host plant or stump and bloom endlessly through the warm weather in fertile, well-drained soil. Shear it to the ground in autumn.

LEONTOPODIUM alpinum
Edelweiss

LEONTOPODIUM

Edelweiss
* **Spring – Summer**
* **Slow/short display**
* **Ht: 20cm/8in/spreading**

After all those years of listening to the 'Sound of Music', one's first sight of the over-romanticized Edelweiss comes as something of a disappointment. I dare say it has some significance to young lovers scrambling about the mountains of central Europe, but that is surely where it should remain. It is not hard to grow in well-drained, gravelly soil in a cool climate, but what have you got? A mound of small narrow green leaves and a short but effective display of greyish daisy flowers, much inferior to the Australian Flannel Flower (see **Actinotus**). The name is Greek, because an ancient writer thought the blooms looked like a lion's foot. Propagate from seed.

LIGULARIA
(syn SENECIO)

☀ ◑ ☀ C T

* **Summer**
* **Fast/long display**
* **Ht: 30-180cm/1-6ft/spreading**

A marvellous daisy genus that is often the highlight of any perennial display — particularly in damp or shaded positions. The **Ligularias** are closely related to the genus **Senecio** and have been included in it by some taxonomists. The general opinion, however, is that they are quite distinct because of the curious way in which the leaf-stalks enclose the main stem, and because of the arrangement of the flower bracts.

These are matters that concern only botanists, and to the rest of us their appeal is in their beautiful foliage and showy heads of golden daisy flowers with strap-shaped petals. Mostly, they are very tall plants, with the exception of the Leopard Plant, **Ligularia tussilaginea,** which is often sold as **L. kaempferi** and a great favourite in Japanese gardens. Grown in full shade, it spreads from an underground rootstock and sends up handsome, shallowly polygonal leaves which may reach 30cm in diameter. These are leathery, and in the popular variety 'Aureo-Maculata' spotted with random yellow blotches, rather like the negative version of a leopard's spots. From time to time in warm weather, it will send up

LIGULARIA przewalski
Chinese Rocket

LIGULARIA dentata

LIGULARIA (continued)

60cm stalks topped with a loose head of pale yellow daisy flowers. **D. dentata,** which has no popular name, is also from the Far East, and a much larger plant, growing generally to 120cm and requiring a spacing of plants up to a full metre. It forms dense clumps of 30cm leaves like those of a giant violet. These are slightly cupped and heavily veined with red or purple. In summer, branched, dark-red flower stems shoot up higher than the leaves and produce large heads of drooping daisy flowers, generally orange in colour. Most striking of all is **L. przewalski,** a stunning waterside perennial from north China, sometimes called the Chinese Rocket. Its long-stemmed 60cm leaves are basically triangular, but deeply and irregularly divided and lobed. Hairy, purple-brown flower stems tower up to 2m, each covered with a dazzling display of sparsely-petalled daisy flowers. The effect is that of a display of blazing rockets shooting skyward from the foliage. All **Ligularia** species can be lifted and replanted from divisions in late spring. They should be cut back to the ground in early winter.

LIGULARIA tussilaginea
Leopard Plant, Farfugium

LIMONIUM latifolium
Sea Lavender

LIMONIUM

Sea Lavender
* **Summer**
* **Average /long display**
* **Ht: 70cm /2½ft /spreading**

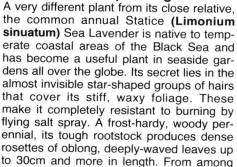

A very different plant from its close relative, the common annual Statice **(Limonium sinuatum)** Sea Lavender is native to temperate coastal areas of the Black Sea and has become a useful plant in seaside gardens all over the globe. Its secret lies in the almost invisible star-shaped groups of hairs that cover its stiff, waxy foliage. These make it completely resistant to burning by flying salt spray. A frost-hardy, woody perennial, its tough rootstock produces dense rosettes of oblong, deeply-waved leaves up to 30cm and more in length. From among them, in warm weather, emerge the many-branched flower stems of papery blue-violet flowers. When fully open, these are so densely covered in bloom they almost hide the plant. **L. latifolium** can be planted out in early spring in any well-drained garden soil, though a sunny position is preferred. If growing plants are not readily available, it is best propagated from root cuttings which are rooted in sandy soil, under glass, in the late winter. Grown on, they may be planted out the following autumn. Seed culture is easy. Just sow the seed indoors, lightly covered with soil, in late autumn. They will germinate in about 3 weeks at a temperature of 21°C/70°F. Plant the seedlings out in spring at spacings of 45cm. In colder inland areas it may be necessary to cut the plants back in late autumn and mulch them.

LOBELIA cardinalis
Cardinal Flower

LOBELIA laxiflora
Torch Lobelia

LOBELIA

Lobelia, Cardinal Flower
* **Summer**
* **Fast/long display**
* **Ht: to 120cm/3½ft**

Lobelias are commonly represented in the garden only by the dwarf blue edging type, yet except for its intense blue colouring it is probably the least interesting of the genus. This includes many of the showiest perennial border plants — about 400 of them, mostly from tropical and warm-temperate areas of the Americas. These taller perennial species like a rich, moist soil, and hold their colour best in a position that is shaded for part of each day. They are not frost-hardy, and in cold areas must be cut back in autumn, dug up and stored under cover until spring when signs of new growth appear. Then, divide, pot up in a peaty mix and water well to stimulate feeding roots before planting out. They can be started from seed in early spring — germination taking about 3 weeks at a constant temperature of 21-24°C/70-75°F. **L. cardinalis** likes damp soil and plenty of water. It has purplish toothed leaves and flat, open flowers of brilliant scarlet. **L. laxiflora** is a woody plant with masses of tubular red and yellow flowers on arching canes and rather narrow foliage. It can be grown in warm-temperate and tropical climates where it will form dense clumps up to 120cm in height.

LUPINUS

Russell Lupin
* **Summer**
* **Fast/long display** ☼ ☀ C T
* **Ht: 1.5m/5ft/spreading**

The ancient Romans called Lupins after Lupus, the wolf, because they were believed to ravage the garden soil. Now we know the opposite is true — crops of annual Lupins are often grown to be dug in and enrich the soil with precious nitrogen. But the glowing Russell Lupin hybrids are a far cry from those European wild species. Raised early in the 20th century by crossing two wild American species, they produce magnificent compound grey-green leaves with up to 17 leaflets, and tall spires of bloom in a rainbow of colours. They like an acid to neutral soil that is not too rich, but must be well-drained. While they can be grown from seed, germinating in about a month, they will not come true to colour, so that named varieties must be propagated from cuttings taken with a piece of rootstock in early spring. These are rooted in sandy soil, potted up and finally planted out in late autumn for bloom the following year. Tall, thirsty plants, they are strictly for the cooler climate, and must be watered heavily, especially in dry weather. Cut faded flower stems to prolong bloom, take the entire plant back to ground level in early winter. Crown rot and powdery mildew can be problems and should be treated with appropriate fungicides.

LUPINUS polyphyllus
Russell Lupin

LYCHNIS chalcedonica
Maltese Cross, London Pride

LYCHNIS

Campion, Catchfly
* **Summer**
* **Fast/long display**
* **Ht: 30-100cm/1-3ft/spreading**

Known and cultivated throughout Europe and Asia since ancient times, the colourful summer-blooming genus **Lychnis** has been through endless reclassification and sorting out so that many plants once included in it are now listed as **Agrostemma, Silene, Coronaria** and **Viscaria.** But the most worthwhile plants of the genus seem still to be included. They grow in any well-drained garden soil (in sun or part shade) but the species **L. chalcedonica** or Maltese Cross will often grow taller, put on a better display where the soil is really moist

in summer. Conversely, they can't bear to become waterlogged in winter, so that poses a bit of a problem. A tall-growing plant (often 1m) with mid-green lanceolate foliage, it bears tall, hairy flower stems topped with flattened heads of orange-scarlet bloom, each with notched petal tips, like a Maltese Cross. The much lower-growing **L. flos-jovis** or Flower of Jove is from the European Alps; the entire plant is a wonderful shade of silver-grey until the brilliant pink or purple flowers appear all over it in loose clusters during the summer months. Very similar is the Rose Campion, **L. coronaria** which makes denser rosettes of an even lighter grey, and somewhat larger single blooms on branched stems held high above the foliage. These are either a vivid magenta shade or white. The German Catchfly, **L. viscaria** (commonly sold as

102

Viscaria) is a useful bedding plant found all the way from Europe to Japan. It bears small green leaves on hairy stems that may reach 50cm in height and spikes of carmine pink flowers that are good for cutting. The double variety 'Splendens Plena' is most often grown. All perennial **Lychnis** species self-seed readily, and should be dead-headed if this is undesirable. A spring mulch and regular water in the flowering season will keep them growing well. **L. coronaria** is relatively short-lived and may be treated as an annual. Seed of most species sown in winter at 21°C/70°F will germinate in less than a month, and plants will flower the first season.

LYCHNIS flos-jovis
Flower of Jove

LYCHNIS viscaria
German Catchfly

LYSIMACHIA

Loosestrife
* **Summer**
* **Fast/long display**
* **Ht: 60-100cm/2-3ft/invasive**

Once grown to repel lice in the pest-ridden Middle Ages, when they were known as 'Louse-strife', all cultivated species of **Lysimachia** are perennial, preferring a moist, loamy soil, and are useful plants for a damp position. They are propagated from autumn or winter divisions and can become quite invasive. A spacing of 45cm is recommended. **L. ephemera** can easily reach 1m, produces tall spikes of star-shaped, pink-centred white blooms in summer. **L. punctata** bears cup-shaped golden flowers arranged in whorls. In rich soil, all species may need twiggy support which will soon be hidden by the flower stems.

LYSIMACHIA ephemera
White Loosestrife

LYSIMACHIA punctata
Garden Loosestrife

MACLEAYA cordata
Plume Poppy

MACLEAYA

(syn BOCCONIA)

Plume Poppy, Tree Celandine
* **Summer**
* **Fast/long display** ☼ ◐ C T
* **Ht: 1.5-2.8m/5-8ft/invasive**

Tallest member of the poppy family by far, the handsome **Macleaya** was named for the early Colonial Secretary of New South Wales who established a spectacular garden in his adopted country. The Plume Poppy (as it is popularly known) is a very tall-growing perennial that should be grown only at the back of a very large border, or on its own among shrubs and trees. Anywhere in fact where there is shelter from strong wind. Fortunately its stems are so thick and tough that staking support is seldom needed. Deep, organically-rich soil is a necessity and lashings of water in the growing season — but be warned, **Macleaya** spreads rapidly from underground roots and can become quite invasive! Set individual plants out over winter at a spacing of 1m at least. The leaves are, quite simply, splendid — 20cm in diameter, deeply lobed and sometimes with a bronze toning on the upper surface. The pinkish buff flowers are very small but appear in profuse panicles at the top of 2.8m stems. The entire plant exudes a uniquely yellow sap when cut, and it should be taken right back to the ground in late autumn.

MECONOPSIS cambrica
Welsh Poppy

MECONOPSIS napaulensis
Pink Himalayan Poppy

MECONOPSIS

Himalayan Poppy, Bastard Poppy
* **Summer**
* **Slow/short display**
* **Ht: 30-200cm/1-6ft**

Many gardeners' hearts have been broken in an attempt to flower these superb hardy perennials, though I remember buying my grandfather a shilling packet of seed for his birthday, and he had no trouble at all. That was half a century ago, when they were a newly discovered wonder of the botanical world. The problem is, that with the exception of the Welsh Poppy **(Meconopsis cambrica,** which will grow anywhere) they must *not* be allowed to bloom the first time they produce buds, for they will then promptly die. They are what is called monocarpic plants, which bloom and set seed once only. But some clever person discovered that if you block the flowering the first year, they'll turn perennial, and bloom for quite a few years in succession. Young plants are sometimes available from mountain nurseries, and should be set out in early spring in a light, rich soil that's shaded and with perfect drainage. It should also be sheltered from wind. Native to high mountain climes, they need plenty of summer water — almost none in winter. The plants may take several years to grow to blooming size, so to avoid disappointment it is recommended you sow seed for several years in succession. This can be done outdoors in autumn for spring germination, or indoors in a seed-raising mix kept constantly at a temperature of 17-21°C/65-70°F. Set the new seedlings out in spring at 30cm spacings and you'll gradually build up a patch of varying-sized plants which should guarantee bloom for some years. But still, the plants are relatively short-lived, and will not last overlong. **M. betonicifolia** and the larger-flowered **M. grandis** produce silky-blue blooms; **M. chelidonifolia, M. dhwojii** and **M. regia** are yellow; **M. napaulensis** is variably pink, purple or white; **M. punicea** deep red; **M. superba** pure white. All are somewhat hairy plants with deeply lobed leaves.

MECONOPSIS betonicifolia ▶
Blue Tibetan Poppy

MIMULUS moschatus
Woolly Monkey Flower

MIMULUS

Monkey Flower, Musk Flower
* **Summer – autumn**
* **Fast/long display**
* **Ht: 20-60cm/8-24in**

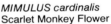

A most variable genus, the majority of **Mimulus** species come from western North America, where they are found wild in moist soils. Hence they are interesting subjects for the low, damp rockery or the boggy wild garden. Seeds of these water-loving perennial plants are sown in late spring, barely covered with the lightest sprinkling of soil mix. Prick them out after germination (about 2 weeks) and plant in their final position early the following spring. They can also be grown from root divisions taken over winter. The perennial **Mimulus** species have a curious clammy feel about them, and of the two illustrated, **M. cardinalis** can be grown in drier conditions or in sun. Both need regular and ample water.

MIMULUS cardinalis
Scarlet Monkey Flower

MONARDA *didyma*
Oswego Tea, Bee Balm

MONARDA *russeliana*
Horse Mint

MONARDA

Bergamot, Bee Balm, Oswego Tea
* **Summer – autumn** ☼ ☀ C T
* **Fast/long display**
* **Ht: 60-100cm/2-3ft/spreading**

In his 1571 book *Joyful Newes out of the New Found World,* botanist Nicolas Monardes introduced an exciting genus of aromatic perennials that was later given his name — **Monarda.** We should gratefully remember him every time we see it grown, smell its fascinating fragrance. There are about a dozen species, all thriving in full sun in damp, well-drained soil. From a tangled mass of running roots they send up square-sectioned stems of mint-like foliage topped in summer with dense heads of tubular flowers surrounded by colourful bracts. These do not come true from seed, so **Monardas** are commonly planted from outer divisions of the root mass in early spring. Plant them in large drifts, and cut back hard in late autumn. Replant every 3 years. Principal colour varieties come in pink, crimson, white and mauve.

MONARDELLA

Pennyroyal
* **Spring – summer**
* **Slow/long display**
* **Ht: 30-40cm/12-16in**

A small genus of North American perennials, closely related to the previously described genus (see **Monarda**), the **Monardellas** are most commonly used in the rock garden or border with light, damp, sandy soil. They can be grown from seed sown *in situ* in autumn, or from spring divisions of the spreading rootstocks which resemble those of the **Monarda.** The stems are noticeably square in cross-section, the leaves narrow, dark and sometimes serrated. The flowers of most species are mauve, pink or white, and borne in dense globular masses, both terminally and at various positions on the stems. **Monardellas** are frost-hardy, but grown mostly in temperate climates where they demand ample water.

MONARDELLA subglabra
Pennyroyal

NICOTIANA tabacum
Tobacco

NICOTIANA

Tobacco
* **Summer**
* **Fast/long display**
* **Ht: 1-1.8m/4-6ft**

'Tobacco's but an Indian Weed' ran an old New England Puritan song which attempted to throw fire and brimstone on the pernicious smoking habit in the 17th century. While the anti-smoking lobby is still in full cry, nobody to my knowledge has yet tried to stop the growing of **Nicotianas,** the decorative plants from which the tobacco leaf is plucked. They are mostly relatively short-lived perennials related to the petunia, and they are best grown from seed, which can be sown indoors in midwinter. Kept at a temperature of 20-30°C/68-86°F, they will germinate in 3 weeks provided they are not covered. After pricking out and potting up, young plants should be set out at spacings of 30cm. They are not frost-hardy, need a rich, moist, well-drained soil.

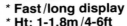

OENOTHERA tetragona ▶
Sundrops

OENOTHERA

Evening Primrose, Sundrop
* **Spring – summer**
* **Fast/long display**
* **Ht: 10-100cm/4-36in**

Colourful perennials for the mixed border or any sunny spot, Evening Primroses mostly open their blooms in late afternoon, suffusing the air with a faint fragrance. As a general name for the genus however, Evening Primrose leaves something to be desired, since some of the most spectacular species flower normally, remaining open throughout the hours of day. These are sometimes referred to as Sundrops, and the showiest of them, 1m tall **Oenothera tetragona,** is shown on the previous page. Like all of the 200 **Oenothera** species, it is native to North America and should be massed in an open, well-drained soil, given plenty of water in the warmer months. It should be planted out from divisions in the colder months, when it has normally been cut back to ground level and is easier to manage. Leaves of the basal rosettes are dull green, generally oval in shape and 20cm in length. As the red stems grow upward, the leaves become smaller and narrower. Golden cup-shaped flowers 3cm in diameter open from scarlet buds. The other illustrated species are much smaller plants, better suited to the rock garden or front of the border. **O. missouriensis** is a dwarf perennial rarely exceeding 15cm in height. Its branched stems are densely clothed with 7.5cm narrow velvety leaves and 10cm yellow flowers that open in the evening for several days in a row; flower buds may be red spotted. The Desert Evening Primrose, **O. californica,** spreads by means of a running underground rootstock which sprouts short stems of hairy, silvery-green foliage at intervals. The leaves are narrow and may be lightly divided or toothed. The flowers are pure white, and open in the evenings from rust-coloured buds, after which they turn pale pink with age. All perennial species of **Oenothera** may be raised from seed sown direct in early spring when the weather has warmed up. Germination should take about 3 weeks. Dwarf species should be spaced about 30cm apart.

OENOTHERA missouriensis
Missouri Primrose

OENOTHERA californica
Desert Evening Primrose

ONOPORDON

Scotch Thistle, Cotton Thistle
* **Spring – summer**
* **Fast/long display** C T
* **Ht: 2m/6ft**

A scourge in many farmers' fields, the ubiquitous **Onopordon acanthium** (better known as Scotch Thistle) is raised in many perennial gardens for its value as a cut flower. The leaves are best described as beautiful but dangerous! They are grey-green, viciously lobed and spined and are best kept well away from paths. The flower heads are another story — reminiscent of the larger **Cynara** (which see) they are typical thistle blooms — 5cm in diameter and tinted a charming pale mauve. **Onopordon** branches heavily to a height of 2m and regular dead-heading will keep it blooming for months as well as reducing indiscriminate self-seeding. Deep, rich soil produces the largest plants, which are easily grown from seed sown directly in the flowering position.

ONOPORDON *acanthium*
Scotch Thistle

ONOSMA *echioides*

ONOSMA

☼

* **Summer**
* **Average/long blooming** C T
* **Ht: 15-45cm/6-18in/spreading**

Said to be most attractive to donkeys, the 190-odd species of **Onosma** are scattered about Europe and Asia Minor, whence a number of them have been adopted into Western cultivation. Like their close relative, borage, they are stiffly hairy plants with bell-shaped flowers borne in the leaf axils. They enjoy a rich, well-drained sandy soil and make splendid plants for the rock garden, since few of them exceed 20cm in height. Nearly all species bloom in shades of yellow, though a few are white, pink and mauve. European **O. echioides** is best propagated from softwood cuttings taken after flowers fade. Root them in sand and peat, then pot up in a good mix until winter's past. Plant out in spring for summer flowers. Seed is slow to germinate.

OSTEOSPERMUM
(syn DIMORPHOTHECA)

Sailor Boy Daisy, Trailing Daisy,
African Daisy, Freeway Daisy
* **Autumn – spring**
* **Fast/long display**
* **Ht: 15-100cm/6-36in/spreading**

Shrubby evergreen perennials related to
the annual **Dimorphotheca** (and often sold
under that name), the **Osteospermums**
make a wonderful display in almost any
garden position of the warmer temperate
climate. They are easy to grow from seed
(sown *in situ* early spring or indoors during
winter if you can maintain a temperature of
16-21°C/60-70°F). First leaves should appear in less than two weeks. Named colour
varieties should be propagated from cuttings or, in the case of **O. fruticosum,** from
rooted sections of the trailing stems. Plant
out in a well-drained position in full sun.
While all species are seen at their best in
good rich soil with regular water, they are
really drought resistant and will continue to

OSTEOSPERMUM ecklonis
Sailor-boy Daisy

OSTEOSPERMUM barberae
African Daisy

OSTEOSPERMUM X 'African Queen'
Freeway Daisy

114

OSTEOSPERMUM fruticosum
as ground cover, California

reward you with a dazzling display of blue-centred daisy flowers through the driest season. Dead-heading will ensure repeat bloom, as will cutting back old spindly branches to thicker wood. Try them spilling over walls or banks, as a low groundcover along driveways or by the pool. **O. fruticosum** is the sturdiest species, spreading at a great rate by trailing branches that root as they go and will easily cover a square metre of space in a single year. The original species is white; colour varieties include mauve 'African Queen', cerise 'Burgundy Mound'. It is a particularly valuable plant in coastal gardens. **O. barberae** and **O. ecklonis** are more shrubby, mounded plants. The former has lilac-pink flowers with deeper-toned reverses, but they close on cloudy days. The latter's blooms are pure white, tinged blue on the reverse. All species can be pinched back to increase bushiness, will flower almost the entire year in a warm, sunny position.

PAEONIA officinalis humilis
European Peony

PAEONIA

Peony, Peony Rose, Moutan
* **Spring – summer**
* **Slow/short display**
* **Ht: 30-100cm/1-3½ft** C T

About 30 species of Peony grow wild right across Asia from southern Europe to Japan. They have been treasured for several thousands of years, and many hundreds of named varieties have come into cultivation. Strictly for areas with a cold winter, Peonies can be divided into two main classes: the shrubby or tree species (which are dealt with in another volume of this series) and the herbaceous species which are shown here. The majority of plants in cultivation (and 3 of the 7 illustrated) are cultivars of Chinese **Paeonia actiflora.** They like a well-drained soil, deeply dug and heavily enriched with well-rotted compost and manure, and resent disturbance once they are established. Planting takes place in the colder months,

PAEONIA mollis
Sweet Peony

PAEONIA lactiflora
'Bowl of Beauty'

except where the soil is frozen, and the crown of the tuberous root mass must be set no more than 2.5cm below the surface. Dress the area liberally with bonemeal, water well and mulch to protect the young shoots as they come through.

Peonies are most effective in mass plantings at 1m intervals, and can be propagated from division of the root mass in autumn. You'll need a really sharp knife for this operation, and must exercise great care if the brittle roots are to escape damage. Make sure each split section includes both roots and dormant growth buds. Peonies can also be grown from seed, though named varieties will not come true. Sow in autumn, prick out late the following spring and grow for 3 or 4 years before planting in the open garden. This is fine for the enthusiast, but a bit slow for the average gardener impatient to see results. Many **P. lactiflora** cultivars have red stems and dark red or purplish foliage. All have beautifully divided compound leaves, sometimes with lobed leaflets. They must be watered deeply and regularly throughout dry weather. Flowers should be dead-

117

PAEONIA (continued)

headed as they fade to prolong bloom and to conserve growing energy which would otherwise be channelled into seed production. Stems are cut back to the ground in autumn. All Peony cultivars are deliciously fragrant and wonderful for indoor arrangements. Stems should be cut just as the blooms begin to open, and laid in a cool place for 24 hours. Then the stems should be lightly trimmed before being immersed up to their heads in water. Leave overnight before arranging. Other herbaceous Peonies should be grown and treated in much the same way. They vary mostly in height and in the complexity of their foliage, which is often fine and fern-like or may have long, attenuated leaf divisions. Unlike the hybrids, they invariably have single blooms. Some taller species may require light staking.

PAEONIA lactiflora
'Bower of Roses'

PAEONIA tenuifolia
Lace-leaf Peony

PAEONIA lactiflora 'Postillion'
Peony Rose

PAPAVER orientale 'Picotee'
Oriental Poppy

PAPAVER

Oriental Poppy
* **Spring – summer**
* **Slow / long display**
* **Ht: 1.2m / 4ft**

☼ C T

Showiest of the poppy genus, and familiar only to gardeners in cold winter areas, are the many hybrids of **Papaver orientale,** the gigantic Oriental Poppy from Armenia. A visitor from warmer climes can only gaze in wonder at the sight of these enormous blooms shrugging away their hairy sepals and unfolding wrinkled, crepe-like petals in the manner of a butterfly emerging from its chrysalis. The petals may take days to reach their full diameter of up to 30cm as a

silken cup brimming with purple-black stamens that protect a many-sided seed-capsule. The fragrance is acrid and somewhat disturbing, as well it may be, for these and other larger poppies are the source of opium and its sinister derivatives. Where the climate is suitable, these magnificent blooms grow from a mass of fleshy roots planted out in autumn in well-enriched, well-drained soil. Preferably the individual clumps should be spaced at 45cm centres for they spread thickly and should not be disturbed for several years. The fleshy roots will begin to produce foliage in late autumn, gradually sending up unbranched stems sparsely furnished with coarse, deeply divided, hairy leaves up to 25cm in length. These stems will really begin to put

PAPAVER (continued)

on growth in early spring, rising 60-120cm according to variety, and in late spring, the plump, furry flower buds appear singly at the end of stems, opening to their full display in early summer. They should be dead-headed as quickly as possible, and may produce a second, smaller flush of bloom in autumn. Otherwise, the foliage will yellow and die down almost immediately, not resuming growth until the following autumn. Because of this unsightly habit at the peak of the perennial season, they are normally interplanted with other species to hide the yellowing foliage. Oriental poppies are short-lived in warmer climates, but elsewhere may be propagated by division of the root-mass in early spring. Named varieties may be multiplied from winter cuttings of outer roots raised in a sandy mixture under glass. They will not come true from seed, but if you wish to experiment, sow indoors at a temperature of 13°C/55°F. Do *not* cover the seeds, give plenty of light, and leaves should appear in two weeks. Bloom cannot be expected, however, in under two years.

PAPAVER orientale
'Perry's White'

PAPAVER orientale
'Goliath'

PELARGONIUM *fulgidum*
Robin Redbreast

PELARGONIUM

Geranium, Pelargonium
* **Spring – autumn**
* **Fast/long blooming** ☼ ☀ T
* **Ht: 30-100 cm/1-3ft/spreading**

To imagine any garden before the 18th century is to see a garden without Geraniums of any sort — and that, today, would seem almost impossible! Is there in fact a garden without at least one of these free-flowering perennials? Blazing away in pots, trailing from baskets, edging borders, spilling over the ground of seaside gardens, even climbing up panels of wire mesh or trellis — their garden uses are without number. And yet, of all the plants illustrated in this book, they have probably been culti-vated for the shortest period of time. The first species of **Pelargonium** (or Geranium

PELARGONIUM X 'Le Quintaux'
Zonal Geranium

121

PELAGONIUM (continued)

as we call them quite incorrectly) did not begin to reach the garden centres of the world until early in the 1700s when the first visitors to southern Africa brought them home as cherished souvenirs. They are so easy to grow that even the most purple-thumbed of gardeners is usually rewarded with success. Water them regularly in summer, lightly in winter; treat them to a weak dose of liquid fertilizer in the growing season — that's all there is to it! You can grow them from seed, of course, and it will germinate in a few days at a temperature of 24°C/75°F — but who would bother when they're so easy to propagate from cuttings? Just tidy up older plants in early spring and insert the cuttings firmly in pots of sand. Pinch out the growing tips as the plants begin to move, allow a few weeks, and plant them out or pot them up. **Pelargoniums** fall basically into two types, those grown for fancy, scented foliage, and those for their flowers. The former are mostly

PELARGONIUM X 'Black Vesuvius'
Fancy-leaf Geranium

PELARGONIUM X 'Henri Joignot'
Zonal Geranium

PELARGONIUM X *peltatum*
Strasbourg Geranium

122

original species, the latter all hybrids. Of these, three types are especially popular.
1. The bushy Zonal Geraniums, classed as **P. X hortorum** hybrids. These have velvety round or kidney-shaped leaves usually marked with a band or zone of contrasting colour. Several varieties are illustrated.
2. The Ivy-leaf Geranium, **P. peltatum** hybrids. These have glossy, fragrant, waxy leaves of ivy shape, and a distinct trailing or climbing habit. **3.** The true **Pelargoniums** or Martha Washington Geraniums, **P. X domesticum** hybrids. These have a spreading, bushy habit, sharply toothed hand-shaped leaves, dark in colour and very fragrant when crushed, and flat heads of larger blooms often beautifully marked in contrasting colours. They have a shorter blooming season, in spring and summer only. None of the **Pelargoniums** is frost-hardy. In cold winter climates they are usually wintered under glass, or cuttings taken and struck indoors, where they are kept till spring. Dead-head all types to prolong bloom.

PELARGONIUM peltatum
Ivy-leaf Geranium

PELARGONIUM X domesticum
Martha Washington Geranium

PENSTEMON

(syn CHELONE)

Beard-Tongue
* **Summer**
* **Fast/long display**
* **Ht: 8-100cm/3-36in**

Most older gardeners will know the common **P. X gloxinioides,** often grown as an annual bedding plant. They may not be so familiar with other species in the genus, native to the western United States. Most **Penstemons** like loose gravelly soil with fast drainage and are splendid in large rock gardens or hillside areas. Even so, they are fairly short-lived. Both **P. davidsonii** and **P. barbatus** (formerly known as **Chelone**) can be propagated from 8cm cuttings of lateral shoots in late summer. Strike these in peat and sand mix, plant out the following spring. Seed can be sown in winter at a temperature of 13-18°C/55-64°F. The former is quite frost-hardy, but **P. barbatus** should be cut back to the ground in autumn.

PENSTEMON barbatus
Chelone

PENSTEMON davidsonii
Mountain Pride

PHLOX paniculata
Summer Phlox

PHLOX X 'Sir John Falstaff'
Perennial Phlox

PHLOX

Summer Phlox, Perennial Phlox ☼
* **Summer – autumn**
* **Average/long display** ☼ C T
* **Ht: 45-100cm/1½-3½ft/spreading**

Another native of the United States, **Phlox paniculata** is one of the most widely grown perennials in cultivation, turning on a dazzling display in many colours. As they spread rapidly into large clumps, **Phlox** are normally set out at spacings of 45-60cm in enriched soil that is both moisture-retentive and fast draining. Water must be kept up at all times if they are to flower well. Dress with a mulch of well-rotted manure in early spring and thin out the weaker-growing stems. Older clumps are thinned out in autumn and the woody inner sections discarded before replanting. Alternatively, cut all growth back hard in autumn and sever young plantlets from the perimeter for replanting. Seed is tricky, should be chilled in the refrigerator for a month before sowing at a temperature of 21°C/70°F. If the seeds are well covered, germination will take a month.

125

PHYGELIUS

Cape Fuchsia, Cape Figwort
* **Summer – autumn**
* **Fast/long display**
* **Ht: 1-1.2m/3-4ft**

C T H

Not related to the fuchsia in spite of its most popular name, the versatile South African **Phygelius** is grown both as an herbaceous perennial and a shrub, the latter in warmer climates. Plant it out in spring, preferably in a sunny position in light, well-drained soil. Space at 60cm to allow room for the rapid, weedy growth. When well fed and watered, the sparsely branched flowering stems will begin to rise in late spring and bloom throughout the summer and autumn. They need no staking in sheltered positions. Seed may be sown in spring, germinating in a few days, but the plants are most easily multiplied from divisions taken at the same time. Cut **Phygelius** back and mulch in colder areas, thin out dead wood elsewhere.

PHYGELIUS capensis
Cape Fuchsia

PHYSOSTEGIA virginiana
Obedient Plant

PHYSOSTEGIA
(syn DRACOCEPHALUM)

Obedient Plant, Gallipoli Heath,
False Dragonhead
* **Summer – autumn**
* **Fast/long display**

C T

* **Ht: 38-110cm/15-48 in/spreading**

Physostegia's giant heath flowers bloom vividly in late summer and autumn. They are good for cutting, but more showy left in the open garden where self-seeding will help them spread rapidly into a dense mass. Plant in late autumn in any acid garden soil, with either full or half sun. The latter seems to produce brighter flower colours. Keep constantly moist in the growing season, and keep them going with a generous sprinkling of pulverized cow manure in spring. They are easily propagated from divisions or from 8cm cuttings of young growth struck in sharp sand. Seed is easy, should be sown outdoors any time in spring and summer. Cut the plants back hard after bloom in late autumn. The popular name Obedient Plant is most appropriate. Flower stems can be bent any which way and will remain where they're put.

126

PLATYCODON

☼ ☀

Balloon Flower, Chinese Bellflower
* **Summer**
* **Slow/long display**
* **Ht: 30-100cm/1-3½ft** [C] [T] [H]

Balloon-like buds swell and pop open into blue star flowers all summer when you've established the charming **Platycodon.** It mixes perfectly with other summer perennials in the open border in all but the hottest districts — then, part shade is best. Plant out autumn or spring at 40cm spacing, then do not disturb after growth begins. While **Platycodon grandiflorum** can be propagated from divisions of the white, fleshy roots, they are best grown from seed, which can be sown outdoors and will germinate in about two weeks at a temperature of 21°C/70°F. Seed should not be covered, and the young plants should be pricked out with great care as they are very brittle. The Japanese have raised single and double varieties in shades of pink, white, mauve.

PLATYCODON grandiflorum
Balloon Flower

POLEMONIUM coeruleum
Jacob's Ladder

POLEMONIUM

Jacob's Ladder, Charity,
Greek Valerian
* **Spring – summer**
* **Fast/long display** ☼ ☀ [C] [T]
* **Ht: 60-100cm/2-3ft**

Few of the 50-odd species of **Polemonium** are in cultivation, and the only one to achieve popularity is the Jacob's Ladder **(Polemonium coeruleum)** which grows wild from England to the Himalayas. It is a charming woodland plant, ideal for the shaded garden, or for naturalizing in moist, leafy soil. Plant it out when dormant, in cold weather, at spacings of 30cm. It needs to be kept moist and should be fed regularly with complete fertilizer as the masses of fibrous roots quickly exhaust the soil. Propagate from seed under glass, and maintain a temperature in the sowing medium of 21°C/70°F, when germination will take about a month. Stems which have borne the panicles of open, mauve, cup-like flowers should be cut right back in autumn. Foliage of all species is somewhat fern-like and collapses fast in dry weather.

POLYGONUM

Knotweed, Snakeweed, Fleeceflower
* **Spring – summer**
* **Fast / long display**   ☼ C T
* **Ht: 15-350cm / 6-144in / rampant**

The 150-odd species of **Polygonum** include some of the world's most rampant weeds — but also some of the most attractive perennial plants with equally rampant habits. Best known is probably dwarf **P. capitatum** which spreads wildly from seed and has running roots which can split a rock. The European Snakeweed, **P. bistorta** has more refined habits, spreading to a dense mat of pointed ovate leaves and sending up 1m spikes of closely packed pink flowers in late spring. A lover of rich, moist soil, it is set out at 60cm spacings in cold weather. Its cousin, the Giant Knotweed, **P. sachalinense,** makes a wonderful screen, may grow 3.5m tall, spreading from underground stems. Cut both species back hard in autumn.

POLYGONUM sachalinense
Giant Knotweed

POLYGONUM bistorta 'Superbum'
Snakeweed, Bistort

POTENTILLA

Cinquefoil, Five Finger
* **Summer**
* **Fast/long display** ☼ ☀ C T
* **Ht: 5-45cm/2-18in/spreading**

Members of the rose family with an extraordinary resemblance to large strawberry plants, the colourful Cinquefoils **(Potentilla** species) include everything from annuals to deciduous shrubs. In the perennial garden, a number of species are grown, ranging from 5cm mat-forming alpines upwards. All have the telltale 5-lobed leaves, and flowers with petals and sepals also in multiples of five. The blooms may be single or double, can be pink, scarlet, maroon, white or yellow. **Potentillas** can be divided in autumn or raised from seed which will germinate in 3 weeks at a temperature of 21°C/ 70°F. Water lightly except in dry weather, feed generously in spring.

POTENTILLA 'Monsieur Rouillard'
Double Cinquefoil

POTENTILLA fragiformis
Scarlet Cinquefoil

PRIMULA

Primula, Primrose
* **Spring – summer**
* **Slow/long display**
* **Ht: 15-100cm/6-40in**

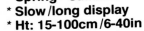

There are more than 500 species of **Primula** found throughout the northern hemisphere and in outlying areas below the equator. They vary widely in style, colour and profusion of bloom, but almost all of them are instantly recognizable for what they are — exotic relatives of the humble European primrose and cowslip. Their height may range to 100cm, their foliage be with or without stems, and borne in a simple rosette from 15 to 60cm across — with individual leaves simple, lobed or toothed and often with a deeply-veined cushiony surface. The flowers, when they appear in spring, are generally in the form of a loose umbel borne at the top of a straight stem, but they may also appear in whorls at intervals along the stem, or in globose heads.

PRIMULA pulverulenta

PRIMULA helodoxa

PRIMULA japonica 'Postford White' ▶
Candelabra Primrose

130

PRIMULA bulleyana

PRIMULA (continued)

They will always, in the wild species, be single, with a tubular corolla flaring into five overlapping lobes, notched at their tips, and with an eye in a contrasting colour. **Primulas** grow to perfection in cooler, moist climates resembling those of their native mountains. Grow them in deep, woodsy soil and preferably in semi-shade. Plant out in the cooler months in a well cultivated position enriched with peat and well-decayed manure. They can be divided and replanted immediately after flowering at spacings relative to the width of their leaf rosettes. Most can be grown from seed sown where they are to grow in early autumn. Even better, sow indoors, after a month's refrigeration on damp seed-raising mix, then suddenly raise the temperature to 21°C/70°F for germination which will take up to 40 days. All need light to germinate so don't cover the seed. Illustrated species are suitable for the shaded garden or border but there are literally hundreds of smaller types for the rock garden or for naturalization. Most **Primulas** grow especially well by water or in boggy ground.

PRIMULA beesiana

PRIMULA nutans
Nodding Primrose

PTILOTUS exaltatus
Mulla Mulla

PTILOTUS

Mulla Mulla, Woolly Bears
* **Spring**
* **Fast/long display**   ☼ T H
* **Ht: 30-100cm/12-40in/spreading**

An uncommon genus of perennials even to native-born Australians, **Ptilotus** includes more than 50 species that thrive in almost desert areas in the north and west of the continent. They make a marvellous display in sunny gardens with perfect drainage, when their loose mounds of softly hairy grey-green foliage suddenly burst into a haze of woolly pink or green flower heads in spring weather. These are deliciously fragrant and borne on long red stems that cut well for decoration. The flowers may be arranged in globular heads or in spikes according to species, and are apparently without petals. Try them in a sandy soil enriched with plenty of decayed manure, and water well from late winter right up to blooming. They need little for the rest of the year. **Ptilotus** may be propagated from short pieces of fleshy root inserted in a sandy mix — or from seed, but germination is rather unreliable. Illustrated **P. exaltatus** will grow to 1m in favourable conditions. **P. spathulatus** bears similar but greenish flower spikes at the tips of trailing stems.

133

PULMONARIA

Lungwort, Spotted Dog
* **Spring**
* **Fast/long display**
* **Ht: 15-30cm/6-12in/spreading**

If this charming genus of perennials had a more pleasant popular name, perhaps we'd remember to grow them more often. For **Pulmonaria officinalis** is perfect for fully shaded areas of the garden in bed or rockery, and develops attractively white-spotted foliage and 2cm pink, bell-shaped flowers that fade to blue as they age. Plant them in any peat-enriched soil in autumn or early spring at spacings of 30cm. They are normally propagated from root division because plants raised from spring-sown seed are said to be inferior. A spring mulch of dampened peat will help to conserve moisture, and they must not be allowed to dry out. Related **P. rubra** has plain green foliage, brick-red blooms.

PULMONARIA officinalis
Jerusalem Cowslip

PULSATILLA X 'Haller'
Pasque Flower

PULSATILLA

(syn ANEMONE)

Pasque Flower
* **Spring – summer**
* **Fast/long display**
* **Ht: 15-60cm/6-24in/spreading**

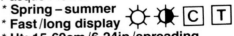

There seems still to be considerable confusion about the nomenclature of these delicate-appearing perennials. In reality, they are tough as old boots and native to cold, mountainous areas of the northern hemisphere. Once included with the **Anemones,** they were renamed **Pulsatilla;** but now, American taxonomists are having second thoughts and have placed them back as **Anemones.** They enjoy humus-rich well-drained soil in open sun and are commonly grown in raised areas of the rock garden. All species have feathery foliage that dies back in winter, and frequently bloom before the leaves are fully developed. Flowers of the illustrated **P.** X 'Haller' are single and commonly a rich purple. As in other **Pulsatillas,** petal fall is followed by rapid enlargement of the flower's sexual parts into a puff-ball of reddish filaments which persists for months.

RANUNCULUS

Buttercup, Crowsfoot, Gold Knots
* **Spring – summer**
* **Fast / long display** ☼ ◑ C T
* **Ht: 30-70cm / 1-2½ft**

The common Buttercup is only one of 250 **Ranunculus** species, largely native to the northern hemisphere but with some alpine species south of the equator. Many species with less rampant growth are popular subjects in the perennial garden. The illustrated Double Buttercup can make a great display in a waterside position, and is propagated from root divisions in autumn. Once established, it will self-seed regularly. The Butter Daisy, **R. gramineus,** on the other hand, is normally propagated by means of seed, which is sown under glass in early spring, pricked out when the grey, grassy leaves are several cm high and set into the garden the following autumn. It is particularly attractive in rockery pockets.

RANUNCULUS acris 'Flore Pleno'
Double Buttercup

RANUNCULUS gramineus
Butter Daisy

REHMANNIA

Chinese Foxglove, Beverly Bells
* **Summer**
* **Fast/long display**
* **Ht: to 45cm/18in/spreading**

Related to such popular annuals as the foxglove, snapdragon and linaria, handsome **Rehmannias** are a small Chinese genus of perennials suited to a wide range of climates. In warm-winter areas they spread rapidly to form large clumps of striking evergreen foliage, the leaves deeply toothed. In colder districts, the plant becomes completely deciduous and dies back. In both places, deep rich soil and plenty of water are needed to produce the tall nodding stems of gorgeous, golden-throated flowers. These may be pink, purple or creamy-yellow according to species, and are splendid for cutting. The most popular species, **R. angulata,** flowers well for several years, then should be replaced, either by means of cuttings or seedlings, which will not bloom until the second year. Sow under glass in winter, when germination will take up to 3 weeks at a maintained temperature of 21-24°C/70-75°F. **Rehmannia** is particularly effective in the shade of deciduous trees.

REHMANNIA angulata
Chinese Foxglove

RHEUM

Ornamental Rhubarb
* **Summer**
* **Fast/long display**
* **Ht: to 2.5m/8ft/spreading**

One of the world's great waterside plants, perennial **Rheum palmatum** is closely related to the edible rhubarb, and makes a stunning display in any moist, deep soil. **Rheums** should be planted at least 1m apart during winter in a position with as much sun as possible, watered heavily and fed with liquid fertilizer at least once a month. The showy, heart-shaped leaves are deeply lobed and reddish-purple when young, changing to green at maturity. They are generally far larger than those of the culinary variety. In rich soil, tall, bracted flowering stems may tower as high as 2.5m with sufficient feeding, each topped with loosely-branched panicles of red bead-like flowers. **Rheum** is propagated from division in the colder months and should be cut back hard in late autumn.

RHEUM palmatum
Giant Rhubarb

RODGERSIA podophylla

RODGERSIA

* **Summer**
* **Fast/long display**
* **Ht: 100-150cm/4-5ft**

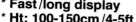

Discovered and introduced to the West too recently to have acquired a popular name, dramatic **Rodgersia** has joined our garden favourites only in the last century. Particularly in waterside areas, its handsome compound leaves with five deeply lobed leaflets introduce a startling colour contrast as they change from green to red during the summer months. There are flowers too, of course, but their interest is secondary — loose sprays of tiny, buff-coloured blooms borne high above the leaves. Plant pieces of the thick, fleshy rootstock 2.5cm below the soil surface during early spring. This soil should be deep, moist and well enriched with decayed compost. Water regularly through the hot weather, cut back flowering stems after bloom.

ROMNEYA trichocalyx
Matilija Poppy

ROMNEYA

Matilija Poppy, Tree Poppy, Fried-egg
Flower
* **Summer – autumn**
* **Fast/long display**
* **Ht: 2-3m/6-8ft/spreading**

'A miracle of loveliness' is one botanical
writer's description of the gorgeous Matilija
Poppy, **Romneya trichocalyx**; Fried-egg
Flower is another less elegant but quite un-
derstandable name for this stunning perennial from southern California. Difficult to
propagate and establish in cultivated gardens, it appears to thrive on neglect in dry,
loose, gravelly soil. Grown from autumn divisions, its grey-green deeply divided
foliage will begin to emerge in winter and
gradually build up to stems 2 metres and
more in height. An occasional deep watering and a mulch of organic material will help
it along, particularly at flowering time, which
lasts for weeks in spring. **Romneya** normally has five or even six petals, each
seeming to be made from snow-white
crinkled crepe. The centre boss of golden
stamens exudes a rich, delicious perfume
and each individual flower may reach 22cm
in diameter. Pick them by all means — they
last for days! Cut the whole plant back hard
in autumn.

138

RUMEX

Rosy Dock, Monk's Rhubarb
* **Spring – summer**
* **Fast/long display** ☀ C T H
* **Ht: to 60cm/2ft/spreading**

Though this colourful perennial grows
widely in outback Australia and makes a
great show in country gardens, it is not native, but has somehow become naturalized
from Egypt and western Asia. Highly recommended for hot, dry areas, it grows as
easily from seed as its rampant relative the
Roving Dock, which can be a terrible pest
when its carroty roots become lodged
under stonework. Sprinkle seed in lightly
cultivated soil — cover, water and stand
back! It'll be up and about in no time,
spreading and sending up hollow stems of
striking heart-shaped 10cm leaves. These
have a mealy surface, and each stem is
topped in warm weather with racemes of
tiny flowers which develop into flat, rosy-red
seed pods. It is also known as Native Hop.

RUMEX vesicarius
Rosy Dock, Native Hop

RUTA graveolens
Herb of Grace, Rue

RUTA

Rue, Herb of Grace
* **Summer**
* **Fast/long display** ☀ T
* **Ht: 60-100cm/2-3ft/spreading**

This fancy-foliaged perennial is one of the
flowers that haunted Hamlet's poor Ophelia
in her madness. A fine, medium-sized addition to any perennial border, it is also grown
in the herb garden, for its finely chopped
leaves add a tangy, bitter flavour to salads.
For cooking, fresh sprigs are snipped, dried
and stored in an airtight container. **Ruta** is
native to southern Europe, and easily
grown from seed sown outdoors in early
spring in lightly cultivated soil. It can be
propagated from 10cm cuttings of lateral
shoots in late summer. These are struck in
a moist, sandy medium, overwintered under
glass and planted out in spring. **Ruta** forms
a dense mass of blueish, finely-divided
foliage from which many-branched stems of
golden buttercup-type flowers emerge in
the warmer months. Rue should be cut
back to old wood in early spring.

139

SALVIA X *superba* 'Lubeck'
Hybrid Sage

SALVIA

Sage
* **Summer**
* **Fast /long display** ☀ ☀ C T
* **Ht: 60-180cm /2-6ft**

Blue, purple, red, white and pink are included in the colour range of **Salvia,** an
enormously varied genus of the mint family,
with which most of them share highly
aromatic spear-shaped foliage. There are
annual, perennial and shrubby species, and
they are scattered in nature all over the
warmer parts of the world. Best known is

the common herb Sage, **S. officinalis,**
which was once credited with medicinal
qualities and thus given the Latin name
salveo — meaning I salve or heal. Though
quite a small plant, it is classed as a shrub
and has many culinary uses together with
the closely related thymes. The perennial
Salvias make superb bedding plants when
densely planted, and are often used by
paths where their foliage, bruised in passing, will exude a spicy fragrance. Three of
the most popular and representative types
are illustrated on these pages. **S. farinacea**
and **S. X superba** are herbaceous perennials and are cut back to ground level in

140

autumn. **S. gesneriiflora,** from Colombia, is classed as a shrubby perennial and develops quite a woody base. All of these demand full sun and grow well in any well-drained soil, though turning on a better display when it has been enriched with well-rotted manure or compost. The herbaceous types can be divided at any time from autumn to spring, and are planted out at the same time at spacings of from 30-60cm dependent on ultimate height. The shrubby types are propagated from 7.5cm cuttings of lateral shoots taken in mid-spring. These should be rooted in sharp sand and peat at a constant temperature of 16°C/61°F, and planted out the following year. All species can easily be raised from seed, though it is not viable for a long period. Sow, uncovered, on a damp medium at 21°C/70°F, and they should germinate within two weeks. Taller growing **Salvias** may need support in exposed positions, but a crisscross of light twigs should be sufficient, and will be hidden by foliage as the plants grow.

SALVIA gesneriiflora
Colombian Sage

SALVIA farinacea
Mealy-cup sage

141

SCABIOSA caucasica
Perennial Pincushion

SCABIOSA

Pincushion Flower, Perennial Scabious
* **Summer – autumn**
* **Fast/long display**
* **Ht: 45-60cm/18-24in**

☼ C T

Wise women of the Middle Ages had a herb to cure every ailment, and with the prevalence of painful scabies, the illustrated flower must have been very popular; it was even named for the disease it was said to cure! Today, **Scabiosa caucasica** is simply a handsome perennial flower planted out in spring for a fine show of delicate mauve or pale blue flowers in the warmer months. It prefers full sun, grows best in fertile, well-drained soil with a ration of lime or dolomite. It can be propagated from basal cuttings in spring, or seed sown at 24°C/75°F under glass. Outdoor sowing in autumn will produce flowers the following summer. The honey-scented blooms on long stems cut well for indoor arrangements. Dead-head regularly, cut back to ground in autumn in cold areas.

SCAEVOLA aemula
Fan Flower

SCAEVOLA

Fan Flower
* **Spring – summer**
* **Fast/long display**
* **Ht: 30cm/12in/spreading**

☼ T

A spreading, sprawling sort of plant, used in mass bedding or as ground cover, the dainty Fan Flower **(Scaevola aemula)** is native to Australia, but was named for the Roman hero Mucius Scaevola, who proved his courage by burning off his right hand. The quaint, lop-sided flowers do in fact resemble a hand as much as they do a fan. **S. aemula** can be grown from seed, but is more usually propagated from cuttings of basal shoots struck under glass. Planted out when rooted at a spacing of 45cm, they spread rapidly into a dense mat. Flowers appear profusely from the red stems through spring and summer, after which the plants can be sheared back to promote spring growth.

SEDUM aizoon
Live Forever

SEDUM

Stonecrop, Rose Root
* **Spring – summer – autumn**
* **Fast/long display**
* **Ht: 7.5-45cm/3-18in**

Though Stonecrops are one of the most popular succulent genera, the majority of them are also frost-hardy, a curious paradox which is due to two factors: 1. They are found naturally in cold winter areas of the northern hemisphere; and 2. When really cold weather kills the succulent foliage, their tough roots can survive beneath the snow, to sprout again the following season. The majority of **Sedums** are low-growing rockery or mat plants, often clinging naturally to almost vertical rock surfaces like the showy dwarf perennial **S. acre** (popularly known as Gold Moss). But the larger species shown in this book grow best in a well-prepared garden soil in full sun — a gravelly mixture suits them best. Spectacular **S. aizoon** can be planted at 25cm intervals, spreads rapidly from tuberous roots to send up heads of starry, golden flowers on 30cm stems in summer.

143

SEDUM (continued)

These are furnished with interestingly toothed, bright green oblong leaves. The more commonly seen **S. spectabile** grows in the same fashion but is much taller. Its foliage is greyish green and the blooms are borne in large flat heads or corymbs of flowers in various shades of pink and carmine. **S. roseum** has distinctly blueish foliage and heads of gold-stamened greenish flowers. Its popular name Rose Root is due to the fact that the dried roots are distinctly rose-scented and may be used in potpourri. All these **Sedum** species can be propagated by cold-weather divisions, or small stem-cuttings struck outdoors in warm weather. They all self-sow readily, but the named varieties do not come true from seed. Water **Sedums** with a light hand — leave the flowered stems over winter and snap them off at ground level in spring to promote new growth.

SEDUM spectabile
Showy Stonecrop

SEDUM roseum
Rose Root

SIDALCEA

Callirrhoe, Checkerbloom,
Prairie Mallow
* **Summer – autumn**
* **Fast/long display**
* **Ht: 70-140cm /2½-4½ft**

Obviously related to hollyhocks, which they greatly resemble, showy **Sidalceas** are altogether smaller plants, growing as low as 70cm, and branching into many flower spikes instead of one spire-like stem. They prefer full sun, need well-drained moist soil and a simple staking with bamboo canes. Plant them in autumn or early spring at 35cm spacings, or divide established clumps in the latter season, replanting only healthy outer growth. Cut flowering stems to 30cm after bloom to encourage a new flush from lateral shoots. **Sidalceas** bloom from summer to autumn and are generally free of problems, although like hollyhocks they do develop rust on the foliage. This is easily treated with fungicide.

SIDALCEA malviflora
Checkerbloom

SOLIDAGO canadensis
Goldenrod

SOLIDAGO

Goldenrod
* **Summer – autumn**
* **Fast/long display**
* **Ht: 30-150cm/12-60in/invasive**

Among the brightest features of North American woodlands in late summer, the handsome, rough-foliaged Goldenrods are easily grown almost anywhere, though they may prove to be relatively short-lived in areas with warm winter climates. There are over a hundred species, of which **Solidago canadensis** is the most commonly seen. They should be planted in colder weather in enriched garden soil and supported with light staking as they grow. Propagation is from divisions of older clumps. Surprisingly, since they bloom in densely-branched plumes of tiny golden florets, they are members of the daisy family, but only close examination with a magnifying glass makes the relationship clear. There are dwarf species for the small garden.

SOLIDAGO X 'Golden Baby'
Dwarf Goldenrod

STACHYS

(syn BETONICA)

Betony, Woundwort, Lambs' Ears,
Lambs' Tongues
* **Spring – summer**
* **Fast/long display** ☼ ☀ C T
* **Ht: 30-70cm/12-30in/spreading**

Commonly used as border edging or
naturalized in light shade, the many attractively foliaged species of **Stachys** are related to mint, sage and other aromatic
plants. Most commonly planted is the lovely
S. byzantina (formerly listed as **S. lanata**)
whose woolly grey leaves are affectionately
known as Lambs' Ears. It does in fact bear
tall spikes of tiny purple flowers in cold
areas, but the foliage is the reason you
grow it. All species are planted in colder
weather, generally from division of older
plants. But seed propagation is also possible, sown under glass at a temperature of
21°C/70°F, when germination will take
about three weeks. Cut flowering stems
back to ground in late autumn; the foliage
will rejuvenate in spring.

STACHYS macrantha
Betony, Woundwort

STACHYS byzantina
Lambs' Ears

STACHYS spicata

STOKESIA

Stokes' Aster, Blue Thistle,
Cornflower Aster
* **Summer – autumn**
* **Average /long display** ☼ ☀ T
* **Ht: 60cm /2ft**

Much admired as a relatively uncommon perennial in English gardens, the beautiful blue **Stokesia** grows like a weed in southern hemisphere climates — quickly spreading by underground stems into a dense clump. Plant them in the mixed border, or in large tubs on your terrace — and please, **do** pick the lovely 10cm daisy flowers! They last well in water, and the picking forces dormant buds into bloom, prolonging the display for months. **Stokesia** is propagated from divisions of the root mass, set out in early spring, or from seed, sown under glass in the cold months at a temperature of 21°C/70°F. You'll get blooms in the first year if you start them early enough, though they may not come true to colour. Mauve is the common variety, but **Stokesias** also come in white, yellow, pink and purple. Sun or light shade suits them, with light watering, and the soil must be well drained. Cut back in autumn.

STOKESIA laevis
Stokes' Aster

SWAINSONA

Swainson Pea, Darling Pea,
Swan Flower
* **Spring**
* **Fast/long display**   ☼ T
* **Ht: 60-100cm/2-3ft/spreading**

A shrubby perennial from outback New
South Wales and Queensland, the Darling
Pea, **Swainsona galegifolia,** makes a colourful show in the dryish garden, provided
the soil is well-drained. Like many another
Australian plant, its seed needs scorching
before it is sown to ensure germination, and
there is a danger it won't come true to colour anyway. The illustrated cerise-red is
common, but the plant may also flower in
mauve, blue, pink, yellow or orange-red.
Safer by far to grow it from cuttings of hardened wood struck in sand. Occasional
water is needed through the warmer
months, and the flexible flowering stems
can be cut back quite hard in late winter.
The blooms are very like those of a sweet
pea, and the shiny leaves are divided into
many leaflets.

SWAINSONA galegifolia
Darling Pea

TANACETUM vulgare
Tansy

TANACETUM

Tansy, Golden Buttons
* **Summer – autumn**
* **Fast/long display**   ☼ C T
* **Ht: 15-100cm/6-36in**

Grown easily from seed or divisions,
species of the small genus **Tanacetum** are
members of the daisy family, and native to
many parts of the northern hemisphere.
Though their flowers are less spectacular
than other daisy-relatives, many of them
are popular in the perennial garden
because of their fernlike, fragrant foliage
and cheerful golden bloom. Not fussy as to
soil, so long as sun and water are available,
T. vulgare is a useful tall plant for the back
of the border, and its leaf-variety 'Crispum'
is a favourite food garnish. Tansy should be
divided and replanted in very early spring,
and the tall flower stems cut back hard in
late autumn. Though it is relatively
trouble-free, aphid infestation can be a
problem.

149

THALICTRUM

Meadow Rue
* **Spring – summer**
* **Fast/short display** ☼ ☀ C T
* **Ht: 60-150cm /2-5ft**

Several species of **Thalictrum** are grown as much for their delicate foliage as for their relatively short-lived flower display. Closely related to the ranunculus and anemone, they sprout from fibrous or tuberous roots and send up tall flowering stems decked with glossy, much divided blue-green leaves having much the appearance of maidenhair fern, or (as in the illustrated **T. aquilegifolium**) of Columbine foliage. They are generally planted from divisions of the root mass in early spring, but take time to re-establish. Single species are better propagated from seed, which will germinate in less than a month at 21°C/70°F. **Thalictrums** look best in light shade, and really thrive in a rich, moist soil that drains well. Staking may be needed, and the plants are cut back hard in late autumn.

THALICTRUM aquilegifolium
Columbine Meadow Rue

THERMOPSIS lupinoides
False Lupin

THERMOPSIS

False Lupin
* **Spring – summer**
* **Fast/long display** ☼ C T
* **Ht: 30-100cm /1-3ft**

Extraordinarily like the North American Lupins (**Lupinus** spp), **Thermopsis lupinoides** is a frost-hardy, herbaceous perennial from Siberia, and is used for a long-lasting display of brilliant golden yellow. While it can be planted from spring division, it may take years to re-establish after the root damage. Better try it from seed which germinates easily in about 3 weeks at a temperature of 21°C/70°F. Seedlings should be pricked out before the heavy taproots become too established and are transplanted to their final position at 45cm spacings in autumn. **Thermopsis** leaves are grey-green, and divided into three sharply-pointed leaflets. Cut the flower stems back after blooming for a second flush. Deep, well-drained soil in full sun is needed for the best effect.

TRADESCANTIA

Virginia Spiderwort, Flower-of-a-Day,
Widow's Tears, Trinity Flower
* **Spring – autumn**
* **Fast/long display**
* **Ht: 60cm/2ft/spreading**

Many species of **Tradescantia** are numbered among popular houseplants, or are used for ground cover in shaded gardens. But the North American **T. virginiana** is quite different, a showy herbaceous perennial with flowers up to 7.5cm in diameter and in a wide range of shades — light and deep blue, mauve, purple, red, soft pink and brilliant white. It is best planted out in the colder months at 45cm spacings, and will rapidly spread into a dense clump, sending up 60cm stems furnished at intervals with pointed, strap-like leaves. The flowers appear in small terminal umbels in spring and early summer, each flower lasting only a day. If the stems are cut back hard, they should bloom again in autumn. **T. virginiana** puts on the best show in moist soil with shade for part of each day. Cuttings strike easily in spring, and seed will germinate readily under glass at a temperature of 21°C/70°F. The dense clumps should be divided in spring every 3 or 4 years.

TRADESCANTIA virginiana
Trinity Flower

151

TROLLIUS ledebourii
Ledebour Globeflower

TROLLIUS

Globeflower
* **Spring – summer**
* **Fast/long season**
* **Ht: 30-70cm/1-2½ft**

Obviously related to common buttercups, the brilliant **Trollius** species share the same needs — a deep, moist soil and a preference for waterside positions. They are propagated from divisions in autumn or early spring and may be raised from seed sown under glass in cold weather. But be warned, it is in no hurry to germinate! Set the plants out at 40cm spacings, water and feed regularly and you can expect a long sequence of bloom. Preferred varieties have double or semi-double yellow blooms, those of **T. ledebourii** flowering in orange shades. Foliage is deeply divided and most elegant.

TROLLIUS europaeus
Common Globeflower

VERBASCUM dumulosum
Dwarf Mullein

VERBASCUM

Mullein
* **Summer – autumn**
* **Fast/long display**
* **Ht: 15-200cm/6-72in**

☀ C T

Tall, stately perennials with many-branched
spikes of open 2.5cm blooms in shade of
yellow, orange, biscuit, mauve and pink,
Verbascum flowers often have contrasting
centres. The plants can be very short-lived
and die off after blooming in their second
year. The only way to be sure of a perennial display is to take root cuttings or sow
new plants each year until they have begun
to self-seed readily. Indoor sowing should
take place within a temperature range of
24-30°C/75-85°F, when germination will be
apparent within three weeks. Tall border
species prefer full sun, and grow in any
normal soil. They are planted out in cold
weather and need staking where they are
exposed to wind. Dwarf alpine species like
illustrated **V. dumulosum** prefer a well-
drained soil and are planted in spring.
Dead-heading of all types ensures continuous bloom.

VERBASCUM X *hybridum*
Mullein

VERONICA

Speedwell
* **Spring – summer**
* **Fast/long display**
* **Ht: 8-60cm/3-24in/spreading**

A large genus with attractive spikes of bloom, the **Veronicas** include annuals, perennials and many shrubby plants from both hemispheres. Dwarf alpine species such as **V. prostrata** spread rapidly to form dense mats of foliage, and are virtually evergreen provided the dead flower heads are trimmed back at summer's end. The taller herbaceous species are planted at 30cm spacings towards the back of the border, and should be cut back hard in autumn and divided every three years. They like a damp, well-drained soil, and the size of their flower spikes is in direct relation to the richness of the soil. **Veronicas** of all types can be raised from seed, which will germinate in about two weeks at 21°C/70°F. Flowers are commonly blue, but pink and white varieties are available.

VERONICA spicata 'Nana'
Spike Speedwell

VERONICA prostrata 'Rosea'
Prostrate Speedwell

VIOLA odorata 'Princess of Wales'
Sweet Violet

VIOLA

Violet
* **Winter – spring**
* **Fast/short display**
* **Ht: 10-15cm/4-6in/spreading**

There seems a great difference of opinion among garden folk as to the position violets prefer, but judging from my own experience I'd say that they are able to organize matters for themselves, and that the poet who placed them 'in a green and shaded bed' was correct. They can spread rapidly, even invasively, from runners and from self-sown seed, and in my garden they always grow most thickly in shaded places, although with good drainage. There, of course, I am speaking of spring-flowering **Viola odorata,** the Sweet Violet in its many colours and forms. Other species such as the dark-foliaged **V. labradorica** definitely prefer shade, and the Australian Native Violet, **V.**

hederacea, blooms best where there is scarcely a ray of sunlight from one month's end to the next. It is widely used as a shaded ground cover by modern landscape designers and seems to bloom all year except (stubbornly) when other violets are in bloom. It is unfortunately not perfumed. Violets then can be propagated by severing young plantlets found at the end of runners; by division of clumps; or from seed. Such seeds will bloom the first year if sown early enough at a temperature of 21°C/70°F, and planted out as soon as possible. But they can also be sown in summer for bloom the following season. By their very name, Violets would be expected to have purple flowers, but there are a lot of lovely species blooming in pink, white, biscuit, pale blue and even yellow. Red spider mites are their worst predator, in dry weather. Spray underneath foliage with miticide, following directions.

ZAUSCHNERIA latifolia
Hummingbird's Trumpet

ZAUSCHNERIA

California Fuchsia, Hummingbird's
Trumpet, Hummingbird Sage
* **Summer – autumn**
* **Average/long display** ☼ C T
* **Ht: 30-45cm/12-18in/spreading**
Sub-shrubby perennials from California, the
Zauschnerias are included in so many
garden books, one suspects, largely because their name begins with Z. It is true
that in their dry, native habitat, where they
bloom late in the season, their scarlet
bloom adds a welcome dash of vivid colour
among the sun-bleached grasses. But with
a profusion of brilliant late-flowering perennials available for the home garden, they
are somewhat overshadowed. Try them in
a dryish, well-drained soil (a raised bed is
ideal) and plant out in late summer. They
are best propagated from spring cuttings of
basal shoots, which can be struck in a
sand/peat mixture. **Zauschnerias** are
evergreen in mild climates, but are cut back
in autumn in cold areas. Prune for shape in
any case.

INDEX

All popular names and synonyms used anywhere
in this book are listed in alphabetical order (with
cross reference to the correct botanical genus,
under which the plants are arranged throughout
the text). Botanical generic names are also included, cross-referenced to the page number on
which each entry commences. Species, named
colour varieties and illustrations will be found
within these alphabetically arranged entries.